Made
—BLAMELESS—

Hal,

Do something dangerous.
Boldly proclaim his name!

Ken

Acts 4:29-30

Ken Kilgore

ISBN 978-1-64471-360-0 (Paperback)
ISBN 978-1-64471-361-7 (Digital)

Covenant Books, Inc.
11661 Hwy 707
Murrells Inlet, SC 29576
www.covenantbooks.com

Preface

The How, Who, and Why

I'm not a writer by trade, although I have always aspired to be. Truthfully, I cannot begin to pull together my thoughts in an orderly manner without the help of God. When I began to write this book, I asked God to help me make sense of what He had heaped up in my brain. He sorted what he had placed there, and I typed.

God has given me so much in this life. He's blessed me over and over again, for reasons I cannot begin to understand. I certainly didn't deserve anything from Him. God is loving. God is willing. God is patient. God is infinitely magnificent and immeasurably great. He proves this to me with each day. It is by His grace that the words that follow are on paper. I believe there is someone in the world that He intends to have read them. I have faith in His purpose.

As a boy, I thought there must be a God. I heard people talking about God. I saw people going to church on Sundays. I even had a grandfather that knew Jesus well. He was a quiet but strong influence on what I now know about God and His beautiful Redeeming Son. I also had people around me that were rough around the edges. They drank, smoked, fought, questioned and, much worse, all in excessive quantity. They clearly were not focused on anything greater than their own wants and wishes. They had good hearts and were loving but were hardened sinners although, in hindsight, probably not that much different than the rest of us. I can't be sure that their names were ever written in the Lamb's Book of Life. They may have known

God but didn't follow Him, at least not outwardly. I pray that, in the end, their pride finally was beaten down by the power of God and they gave themselves to Him fully. I hope that I see them all in heaven.

Unfortunately, I possess a self-reliant spirit too. My trouble has always laid in my arrogance and pride. Both have been the root for many different sins to sprout and excessively grow. At times in my life, sin has been an infestation. God has had to cut away some branches. With a stomp of His boot, He has abruptly broken out the worthless upshots. And so too He has delicately pruned what may have shown Him some promise. My eyes have been opened, and now I see His light. I thank God for loving me enough to cut this world out of me. To His glory, I am thankful that He has thrown those worthless branches into the fire. I'm thankful too that He is a gardener that doesn't ever give up. I have grown so much with His nurturing. I'm His now. He can sculpt and shape me anyway He wants. I trust Him.

I want to thank my wonderful wife, Mary. Truly, it was her example and love that showed me how to open my Bible and eventually accept Jesus Christ as my Savior. Without her, I don't believe that I would have ever surrendered before the cross. Her examples of standing firm in the face of a difficult world and trusting God, no matter what His response, have been a perfect compass for me. I know that God works through her often. He knows He can count on her. What an amazing gift she has shown me—eternal life in heaven with the God who loves us.

When I started to write what follows, I wasn't sure why I was doing it. I was being led to put some words down in hope that someone might read them! I am prayerful that readers will be encouraged to immerse themselves in their Bible and that a few may even find Jesus through the words. My hope too is that my three sons and their families might someday be inspired to learn how the amazing power and grace of Jesus Christ can transform them. I pray that God's word will always be known to them and that the Holy Spirit will fill them up to overflowing. "You will seek me and find me when you seek me with all your heart. I will be found by you," declares the Lord…" (Jeremiah 29:13, NIV).

Know that God loves you. He loves you no matter what you have said or done or how often you have done it. If you accept that the blood of Jesus, His Son, was shed on the cross as payment for your sins, and ask Him to come into your life, you will be changed forever! God is perfect in His grace and forgiveness. His Holy Spirit will always be with you and will lead you!

"And I will ask the Father, and he will give you another Counselor to be with you forever—the Spirit of truth. The world cannot accept him, because it neither sees him nor knows him. But you know him, for he lives with you and will be in you" (John 14:16–17, NIV).

If you already have accepted Jesus as your Lord and Savior, I pray that this book will strengthen you to live boldly for Him! If you haven't bowed your knee in front of Jesus yet, His love and joy and offer of everlasting life is waiting for you!! Seek Him and you will find Him!

Contents

After reading, please give this book to a friend or family member that may need encouragement to come to Jesus!

For further comments or questions, please feel free to correspond with the author directly by email at kilgorekenj@gmail.com

For we ourselves were once foolish, disobedient, led astray, slaves to various passions and pleasures, passing our days in malice and envy, hated by others and hating one another. But when the goodness and loving kindness of God our Savior appeared, he saved us, not because of works done by us in righteousness, but according to his own mercy, by the washing of regeneration and renewal of the Holy Spirit, whom he poured out on us richly through Jesus Christ our Savior, so that being justified by his grace we might become heirs according to the hope of eternal life. (Titus 3:3–7, ESV)

He Who Overcomes

There is always a challenge ahead of us or an adversity we have to face—the overdue house payment, the bottom line, that pesky credit card debt, the messy house, laundry, a boss that's impossible, a roof that needs repaired, and sometimes just getting up in the morning to face it all. Oftentimes, we find ourselves caught up in a daily battle just to overcome life's "necessary evils." On top of all of that, we are trying to climb the corporate ladder, get a raise at work, save for retirement, and read the latest self-help book on how we can become a better manager or parent. Some of us are even overachievers who passionately fight every day for a cause like equal rights, environmental awareness, cultural acceptance, or just trying to tip our corner of the world toward becoming more conservative or progressive. You have to wonder sometimes if we're supposed to put forth so much effort to juggle all of these balls. It's hard most days just fitting it all in twenty-four hours and getting any sleep! Are we falling into a pit too deep to climb out of? Are we trying to accomplish too much, or are we just driven to achieve the wrong objectives?

The famous actress, Katharine Hepburn, said, "Life is hard. After all, it kills you." Life is not hard, but it is a minefield of sorts set by the devil. We are seduced by misdirection and diversions designed by the evil one to lure us off salvation's path. Satan cleverly dangles big houses, new cars, and exciting vacation packages in front of us, effectively making us foot soldiers for the wrong cause. When we are struggling to improve ourselves, or fighting for a social or political cause, or paying for last year's trip to Cancun, we are tragically spending our time and effort on what will not result in our eternal salvation. We allow ourselves to be drawn off the right path and into "the valley of the shadow of death." The devil wants us bogged down chest deep in the muck and the mire of this world instead of seeking the face of God to shine on us and restore us.

Instead of being a slave to this world, we can overcome it.

> For everyone who has been born of God overcomes the world. And this is the victory that has overcome the world—our faith. Who is it that overcomes the world except the one who believes that Jesus is the Son of God? (1 John 5:4–5 ESV)

When you overcome this world by faith in Jesus Christ, you will no longer be under the influence of Satan's temptations. You will begin following a different path and a different shepherd. Things that were once necessity will become trivial. There will be no more seduction, no more lies, and no more snares. You'll walk out of the muck and into the arms of a God that loves you and has been waiting for you! God will set your feet upon the path that leads to eternal life through The Son. He will make your way easy. "I will go before you, and level the mountains" (Isaiah 45:2, NIV).

In the book of Revelation, John was asked by the son of man to "write on a scroll what you see and send it to the seven churches." There was much promised for "those who overcome."

"To him who overcomes, I will give the right to eat from the tree of life, which is the paradise of God" (Revelation 2:7, NIV). When you have made the choice to overcome, you are not only promised eternal life but given the righteousness of God and a stately dwelling in His perfect paradise!

"He who overcomes will not be hurt at all by the second death" (Revelation 2:11, NIV). As followers of Jesus, we were baptized into His crucifixion and also into His resurrection. In the end, God will slay the unbelievers forever, but those who believe will enjoy everlasting life! Death will come upon us once, but after that, death will have no relevance to those who overcome.

"To him who overcomes, I will give some of the hidden manna. I will also give him a white stone with a new name written on it, known only to him who receives it" (Revelation 2:17, NIV). When you have accepted Jesus as Lord, all of the plagues of your past are forgiven. Whoever you were and whatever you did is covered by the righteousness found only in the Savior. You are pardoned forever by the righteous act of Jesus—the blood he shed to make us blameless. Throw away your old name along with your secrets and sins. You'll have a new name—a saintly one.

"To him who overcomes, and does my will to the end, I will give authority over the nations-he will rule them with an iron scepter; he will dash them to pieces like pottery-just as I have received authority from my father. I will also give him the morning star" (Revelation 2:26–28, NIV). Those who overcome will have authority over demons, disease, and sin. We will reign alongside Jesus, and with the power given to us by God, our overwhelming strength will crush evil.

"He who overcomes will, like them, be dressed in white. I will never blot out his name from the book of life, but will acknowledge his name before my Father and his angels" (Revelation 3:5, NIV). When you overcome, you are given eternal salvation. You are made new in Christ. Saved by His grace, you will not fail. His gift of grace is secure forever, and He will finish His good work in you. God will always speak your name. He will know you completely, and you will know Him.

"Him who overcomes I will make a pillar in the temple of my God. Never again will he leave it. I will write on him the name of my God and the name of the city of my God, the new Jerusalem, which is coming down out of heaven from my God; and I will also write on him my new name" (Revelation 3:12, NIV). Followers of Christ will forever be in the sight of God. As Jesus is in God, we will also be. We will forever feel His love and live in His glory. "They will be His people, and God himself will be with them and be their God" (Revelation 21:3, NIV).

"To him who overcomes, I will give the right to sit with me on my throne; just as I overcame and sat down with my Father on his throne" (Revelation 3:21, NIV). As one that has overcome, you will sit with Jesus on the throne! You are part of the kingdom—a son of God, a brother of Jesus, an ambassador, an heir. No matter what you have done, your repentance has made you royalty!

"He said to me: 'It is done. I am the Alpha and the Omega, the Beginning and the End. To him who is thirsty I will give to drink without cost from the spring of the water of life. He who overcomes will inherit all this, and I will be his God and he will be my son'" (Revelation 21:6–7, NIV).

Life doesn't have to be hard. It's our own fault if it is. We step in the snares when we chase the shiny trinkets being dangled by the devil. Through well-disguised trickery, Satan grows closer to gaining our soul with every second that ticks away. Evil works diligently to divert our attention away from seeking God, keeping us from giving ourselves to Him who loves us.

We can overcome this world and all of its struggles in one bold move. All we need is to fall at the feet of Jesus, ask for forgiveness, and then get up and follow Him. If we place all of our effort on seeking God, locking our eyes solely on our Lord and Savior, our yoke will be made easy (reference Matthew 11:30, NIV). When you have the Son and the redemption found in His grace, this world will just fall into place. You won't need self-help to become a better parent; you'll be one. You won't have to work hard to better your career; success will have new meaning. You won't have to struggle with that personal flaw or addiction; He'll fix that. You won't spend time fighting for anyone's rights; you'll be busy showing them the way. You'll trade next year's warm beach for introducing revival in your neighborhood. They who unswervingly seek the awesome power of God will overcome all of the misdirection, diversions, and snares. In doing so, God will level the mountains for you and you will sit on the throne forever. Royalty!

Where are You?

The woman was convinced. She saw that the tree was beautiful and its fruit looked delicious, and she wanted the wisdom it would give her. So she took some of the fruit and ate it. Then she gave some to her husband, who was with her, and he ate it, too. At that moment their eyes were opened, and they suddenly felt shame at their nakedness. So they sewed fig leaves together to cover themselves.

When the cool evening breezes were blowing, the man and his wife heard the Lord God walking about in the garden. So they hid from the Lord God among the trees. Then the Lord God called to the man, "Where are you?"

He replied, "I heard you walking in the garden, so I hid. I was afraid because I was naked."

Who told you that you were naked?" the Lord God asked. "Have you eaten from the tree whose fruit I commanded you not to eat?" (Genesis 3:6–11, NLT)

God has been searching, asking, "Where are you?" Are you hiding from Him? Are you keeping sins hidden from Him and from those around you? What are you hoping no one will see? Nothing is hidden from God. He searches the earth ceaselessly for those who are lost. He lays secrets to bare and carves disgrace from hearts. He dismantles the proud and rebuilds the broken. He is hope for the downtrodden. He is freedom for the trapped. Those "whose hearts become completely His" will be clothed in His strength and glory. They will be made fearless by His mercy and forgiveness!

"For My eyes are on all their ways; they are not hidden from My face, nor is their iniquity concealed from My eyes" (Jeremiah 16:17, NASB). Hiding is just nonsense. Why not reveal what He already knows? Why not ask Jesus to place His seal on our lives? Take the first step onto the way that is right. Kneel in prayer and clear the rubble from your path. Confess your wrongs to Him. Surrender to Him those things that enslave you. Hammer them into the cross with the nails that held His hands and feet. "God made you alive with Christ. He forgave us all our sins, having canceled the charge of our legal indebtedness, which stood against us and condemned us; he has taken it away, nailing it to the cross" (Colossians 2:13–14, NIV).

Living in Jesus, He erases all of the ugliness from view. God sees us dressed in the perfect image of our Savior. He finds us faultless. "Even before he made the world, God loved us and chose us in Christ to be holy and without fault in his eyes" (Ephesians 1:4, NLT). It's like hiding in plain sight, shielded by the light of the Son. "As for God, his way is perfect: The Lord's word is flawless; he shields all who take refuge in him" (2 Samuel 22:31, NIV).

God is calling out. He's forever faithful in His love. There is no need to hide. He's ready to shoulder your burdens. He's offering His hope and mercy. Where are you?

Who Do You Say I Am?

Considering his own talents, Vincent van Gogh had incredible praise for Jesus. In 1888, in a letter to fellow artist Emile Bernard, the acclaimed artist referred to Jesus as "an artist greater than all artists."

> He lived serenely, as a greater artist than all other artists, disdaining marble and clay as well as color, working in living flesh. This extraordinary artist—Christ—hardly conceivable with the obtuse instrument of our nervous and stupefied modern brains, made neither statues nor pictures nor books; he loudly proclaimed that he made... living men, immortals. (Vincent van Gogh)

For more than two millennium now, this world has referred to Jesus Christ as many different things. John the Baptist referred to Jesus as "the Lamb of God who takes away the sin of the world" and "the Son of God" (John 1:29–34 ESV). "And he preached, saying, "After me comes he who is mightier than I, the strap of whose sandals I am not worthy to stoop down and untie" (Mark 1:7 ESV). The apostle John, in his greeting to the Seven Churches, spoke of Jesus as "the faithful witness, the firstborn of the dead, and the ruler of kings on earth" (Revelation 1:5, ESV). The prophet Isaiah referred to Jesus as our "wonderful counselor," the "Prince of Peace," and our "Mighty God." He also identified Him as our "Everlasting Father," perhaps further defining John's name of "the firstborn of the dead,"—the first to be resurrected into everlasting life. As Christians, our hope after death is to join Jesus in heaven, newly born into eternal life.

Jesus made it known that He is interested in how we describe him, who we believe Him to be, and how we accept the One who will intercede on our behalf (reference Isaiah 53:12). "'But what about you?' he asked. 'Who do you say I am?' Simon Peter answered, 'You are the Christ, the Son of the living God'" (Matthew 16:15–16, NIV). When you go before the throne on judgment day, the answer to the question will already be known. There will be a replay of those transcending opportunities we were given throughout life to answer the question, "What about you? Who do you say I am?"

Job called Him his Redeemer. "I know that my Redeemer lives, and that in the end he will stand upon the earth. And after my skin has been destroyed, yet in my flesh I will see God; I will see Him with my own eyes—I, and not another" (Job 19:25–27, NIV).

Paul spoke of Jesus in 1 Thessalonians 1:10 ESV as the Deliverer. "…his Son from heaven, whom he raised from the dead, Jesus who delivers us from the wrath to come." Also, in his letter to Titus, Paul referred to Jesus as "the blessed hope," and "our great God and Savior." "For the grace of God that brings salvation has appeared to all men. It teaches us to say NO to ungodliness and worldly passions, and to live self-controlled upright, and godly lives in this present age, while we wait for the blessed hope—the glorious appearing of our great God and Savior, Jesus Christ" (Titus 2:11–12, NIV).

As the very end of times unfold, the book of Revelation describes Jesus as "there before me was a white horse, whose rider is called 'Faithful and True.' With justice he judges and makes war. His eyes are like blazing fire, and on his head are many crowns. He has a name written on him that no one knows but he himself. He is dressed in a robe dipped in blood, and his name is the Word of God" (Revelation 19:11–13, NIV).

Driven by saving souls, and in tireless and faithful ministry, Jesus answered His own question many times, "Who do you say I am?" In Revelation 1:8 (NIV), Jesus spoke of himself as "I am the Alpha and the Omega," says the Lord God, "who is and who was, and who is to come, the Almighty." In John 8:12 (ESV), "Again Jesus spoke to them, saying, "I am the light of the world. Whoever follows me will not walk in darkness, but will have the light of life." And also in John 11:25–26 (ESV), Jesus said, "I am the resurrection and the life. Whoever believes in me, though he die, yet shall he live, and everyone who lives and believes in me shall never die. Do you believe this?"

After washing the feet of His disciples, Jesus prepared the group for what was to come—His arrest and crucifixion. He comforted them by saying, "I will come back and take you to be with me that you may also be where I am. You know the way to the place where I am going" (John 14:3–4, NIV). His disciple Thomas said to him, "Lord, we don't know where you are going, so how can we know the way?" Jesus answered, "I am the way and the truth and the life. No one comes to the Father except through me. If you really knew me, you would know my Father as well. From now on, you do know him and have seen him" (John 14:5–7, NIV).

It all came down to that for those first disciples who loved Jesus. They had given everything to follow Jesus. They had left families, homes, businesses, and inheritances. They had been persecuted already, and they knew the worst was yet to come as they continued the ministry. Before becoming "fishers of men," they had everything in this world they needed. Now though, Jesus told them that he would be leaving to join the Father. The disciples would be gathering the harvest without Him. As they did, Jesus would be preparing a place for them in the Father's house. To paraphrase, the disciples were told, "Relax…when the day comes for you to come home to the Father…you know the way." It was Jesus's most prolific statement. It answered the question "Who do you say I am?" Jesus said, "I am the way." Jesus said, "I am the truth." Jesus said, "I am the life."

How is Jesus "the way?" He said that "No one comes to the Father except through me." He is not just "the way," He is "the only way." Today, Christians are expected to be tolerant of those who follow other faiths and worship other gods. The world cannot afford that sort of kindness. The stakes are too high. Tolerance does not save souls. Instead, we should proclaim the name above all names to everyone we meet—the true and only path, so no one is lost. "Salvation is found in no one else, for there is no other name under heaven given to men by which we must be saved" (Acts 4:12, NIV).

"This is how God showed his love among us: He sent his one and only son into the world that we might live through him" (1 John 4:9, NIV). It's simple really. Anyone who does not love and follow Jesus Christ needs a "come to Jesus" intervention, or they should prepare to be cast into the fiery lake.

When Jesus said He was the truth, He meant it literally. Emphasis on the word "the." He didn't mean that, verbally, his words were the "truth" or the words written about Him in the Bible were the "truth," although they certainly were. He meant that he was Truth, as in, the embodiment of truth. "So Jesus said to the Jews who had believed him, 'If you abide in my word, you are truly my disciples, and you will know the truth, and the truth will set you free'" (John 8:31–32, ESV). Jesus was Truth in person. Remember the white horse mentioned earlier in Revelation 19? Its rider was called "Faithful and True." The blood that His robe was dipped in was the price He paid on our behalf. Jesus bore the blood. The angels were made pure in white. If you are a disciple of Truth, then you are no longer a slave to sin. "For the law was given through Moses; grace and truth came through Jesus Christ" (John 1:17, NIV).

Life comes from Jesus Christ. It did in the beginning. It does now. It always will. Jesus is in us and we are in Him. "Through him all things were made; without him nothing was made that has been made. In him was life, and that life was the light of men" (John 1:3–4, NIV). Through Jesus, we have been given love, hope, mercy, forgiveness, joy, and trust. By His grace, we are redeemed. He is our breastplate of righteousness. Through Jesus we have faith in what we cannot see. Our resurrected Savior lives forever…and so will we!

Jesus asked Peter a vitally important question. He asks the same question to all of us. Your eternal life depends on how you answer— Jesus is asking, "Who do you say I am?"

Sources:

Van Gogh quote: www.vangoghletters.org #632 To: Emile Bernard Tuesday June 26, 1888

Sharpening Warriors

> I have worked much harder, been in prison more frequently, been flogged more severely, and been exposed to death again and again. Five times I received from the Jews the forty lashes minus one. Three times I was beaten with rods, once I was stoned, three times I was shipwrecked, I spent a night and a day in the open sea... I have labored and toiled and have often gone without sleep; I have known hunger and thirst and have often gone without food; I have been cold and naked... (2 Corinthians 11:23–27, NIV)

Paul spoke all of this as if it were "boasting." In fact though, history would confirm that Paul was being quite honest, and to some extent, humble. His sufferings, while for the gospel of Jesus Christ, were even worse than what he described in his letter to the Church of Corinth. When Paul received *"forty lashes minus one,"* he was whipped with a leather strap containing three thongs, so for each of the five punishments, the Jews actually handed out triple the lashes. Paul also listed that he had been stoned. In fact, he had been stoned as punishment for "blasphemy" by the Jews in Lystra, where he was so badly pummeled that he was left for dead (reference Acts 14:19–20). Paul failed to list betrayal, arrest, attack by wild beasts, snake bite, robbery, sickness, burns, and many other sufferings. Paul was eventually beheaded outside Rome in 67 AD, after being imprisoned once again for his faith. Paul was no stranger to hard times.

Many of us have also known difficulties. Today, although we can experience troubles of many sorts, it is not typical for our lives to be at risk for our faith in Jesus Christ, nor are we too often endangered by wild beasts or snakes, nor are we flogged, beaten with rods, or living naked outside. We do experience horrific accidents sometimes though, and we do fight for our very life from time to time with serious health battles. Most all of us know or have family members who are stricken with challenges and afflictions. There are any number of diseases or illnesses that claim human life every day. As if that weren't enough, there are traffic accidents, workplace accidents, or just "freak accidents" that can change lives forever. How should we live with sickness or afflictions? How should we feel about a life altering accident?

Paul taught that, in hardships, we grow closer to God. He understood that the Sculptor could choose to mold the clay in ways we may not understand, and sometimes, the blind were made to see in terrifying yet fortunate ways (see Saul's Conversion in Acts Chapter 9). Knowing this, Paul rejoiced in his difficulties! "We rejoice in the hope of the glory of God. Not only so, but we also rejoice in our sufferings, because we know that suffering produces perseverance, perseverance, character; and character, hope. And hope does not disappoint us, because God has poured out his love into our hearts by the Holy Spirit, whom he has given us" (Romans 5:2–5, NIV).

Isaiah prophesied on 'The Suffering and Glory of the Servant,' saying, "He was despised and rejected by men, a man of sorrows, and familiar with suffering" (Isaiah 53:3, NIV). He went on to add, "After the suffering of his soul, he will see the light of life, and be satisfied…" (Isaiah 53:11, NIV). And also, "Therefore I will give him a portion among the great, and he will divide the spoils with the strong, because he poured out his life unto death, and was numbered with the transgressors" (Isaiah 53:12, NIV).

In Hebrews 2:10, it is said that God made Jesus "perfect through suffering." Then, "Both the one who makes men holy and those who are made holy are of the same family. So Jesus is not ashamed to call them brothers" (Hebrews 2:11, NIV).

Finally, Peter wrote, "Therefore, since Christ suffered in his body, arm yourselves also with the same attitude, because he who has suffered in his body is done with sin. As a result, he does not live the rest of his earthly life for evil human desires but rather for the will of God" (1 Peter 4:1–2, NIV).

A saying from today's world states that "iron sharpens iron." Overcoming trials and tribulations makes us stronger. Our God uses suffering, sickness, persecution, rejection, and hardship to sharpen us as a warrior for Christ!! Jesus willingly suffered for us and now calls us "brothers." If it has been God's will to cause struggle to the point of suffering in your life, although incredibly difficult to bear, we must consider it a blessing. Through your suffering, you are now living for the will of God, a brother alongside Jesus Christ. The struggle may not become easier, but the reward will be forever, "a portion among the great!"

Tony

Tony was standing at the door of the Eagle Truck Stop Restaurant in New Philadelphia, Ohio. I was there on business, and apparently, so was Tony. It was a dry day with the temperature hovering just above freezing. He was dressed in blue jeans and had on several layers of coats with a New York Yankees ball cap atop his head. He had short graying hair and was freshly shaven. He was missing a few front teeth, but his clothes were clean and unwrinkled. Tony opened the door for me, greeting me with "Good morning sir! Do you know Jesus?" Before I could answer, he quickly followed with "He can be a friend when you really have no one else. He was the Son of God, and He gave his life for you because He wants you to live forever with Him in heaven someday."

At first, I thought Tony was homeless and was just going to ask me for a few dollars. He didn't. Instead, after he spoke, there was an awkward silence as he waited for my answer. He sincerely was asking for something far more valuable than money. Tony was an eternity planner.

I explained to him that I actually already had a relationship with our Lord and Savior. I told him that I pray many times each day, and that I've been studying my Bible closely for years. Then I asked him his story.

"I learned about God and Jesus in prison," he said, with his eyes pointed toward the sidewalk. "I was in a medium security prison in Lima, Ohio, when I was saved by a preacher that was sharing the gospel while visiting inmates. God found me when I was so low that I had nothing to lose. I was good for nothing, yet God still wanted me." He continued to testify, "I didn't have any family that loved me. No one wrote to me. I was alone and behind bars. I found friendship in Jesus Christ, and I learned how much Jesus loved me. From that point on, I studied my Bible nonstop. I joined other prisoners in nightly Bible study. I gave my life to Jesus right there in a dark prison cell one night. It was the greatest moment of my life. I remember being filled with this feeling of warmth. I belonged to something. God told me I was going to be a missionary that same night. I didn't even know what that meant! I didn't know how He planned to use me, but I felt needed!"

His testimony had my full attention. I pried him for more. He continued, "I was released fifteen years ago. I started traveling the country by foot and by free rides—some from strangers, and some from brothers in Christ. I share the gospel with anyone that is interested in listening. It's my job. I can barely sleep at night because I'm so excited about getting up the next day and talking to more people." Then he showed me the small Bibles that he freely gave away to those that showed real interest.

As people filed in and out of the restaurant, Tony opened the door for them too, saying, "God loves you. Have a wonderful day." If someone spoke back, he followed up sharply, "Find some time today to read your Bible. Read the book of Romans, chapter 5. If you need a Bible, I'll give you one!" He was met mostly with ignoring eyes that turned away.

Others said, "Thank you."

A few others seemed sincere when they said, "Thanks, I'll do that."

Tony lived on the road and carried everything he owned. He had no house or house payment, no insurance, no car, no cell phone, no bank account, no credit cards, and no safety valves. He was truly walking the country completely dependent upon God to protect and provide for him. Tony was living no differently than the first disciples did when they spread the gospel of Jesus Christ to the world. He relied on the goodness of others for shelter, food and drink, clothing, and for cash to replenish his inventory of Bibles to put in the hands of new found believers. He carried his life in a backpack. It was everything he had and everything he needed.

He liked to travel between truck stops. Showers and a laundromat kept him visibly acceptable and, therefore, relevant. He said that his backpack doubled as his pillow, but oftentimes, the people he had met provided him a place to sleep. Sometimes, if he saw that they needed help, or if they had pressing work to be done at their homes or businesses, he would stay and help. He had made a network of friends along his path and revisited them occasionally just as the Apostle Paul had done two thousand years ago, "for the purpose of strengthening and uplifting the believers."

I talked to Tony for nearly an hour. At one point, I pulled forty dollars from my wallet and tried to give it to him. He refused! He said, "I'm not a panhandler. If you want to give to my ministry though, I will accept up to twenty dollars. I have a limit set. I split offerings; fifty-fifty. I use 50 percent to purchase Bibles. I use the other 50 percent for food, or laundry, or to help people who need it worse than I do." When I asked why there was a limit set, he responded, "I'm afraid I won't use it as God intended if people give me too much. I don't want to fall into wanting things that I don't really need. That caused problems for me in my earlier life." I was taken back. This man was truly living for God. This man wasn't living on the street. He was evangelizing the streets as a modern-day apostle. I could not help but be reminded of how the angel Gabriel described what John the Baptist would become to his father, Zechariah. Gabriel described him as "he will be great in the eyes of the Lord," and "he will be a man with the spirit and power of Elijah. He will prepare the people for the coming of the Lord. He will turn the hearts of fathers to their children, and he will cause those who are rebellious to accept the wisdom of the godly" (Luke 1:5–25, NLT). God surely felt the same way about this man.

I stood by as he spoke to a young mother with two daughters. It was obvious that life was a struggle for her. He told her about some of the struggles Jesus, the very Son of God, had experienced—persecution, hatred, criticism, temptation, rejection, betrayal. Then he told her about Jesus's death on the cross, and what it meant for her if she chose to believe in Him. He told her how the early followers of Jesus Christ had all of the same challenges she had today—how they also were feeding families, working to keep a place to live, to keep warm, and to pay the bills. I could tell that his words resonated with her. He gave her a Bible with post-it notes marking a few pages. He told her, "This is just the New Testament. It's the part about Jesus—the most recent stuff. I hope you read all of this, but please, at least read the parts I have marked for you. If you read this and believe it, then pray to Jesus. Ask Him for forgiveness for all of the wrong things you have done. Ask Him to come into your life and good things will happen for you. I'm living proof." I believe that he saved a soul right there in front of me. He was powerful. This wasn't just a man speaking. God was working through him—giving him the words. He was perfect in his delivery. He revealed to her his sincerity and goodness. She saw that he cared about her future. I have no doubt that she went home and read until she prayed. The Holy Spirit gave that woman new life.

In his letter to Philippi, Paul wrote "whatever were gains to me I now consider loss for the sake of Christ. What is more, I consider everything a loss because of the surpassing worth of knowing Christ Jesus my Lord, for whose sake I have lost all things. I consider them garbage, that I may gain Christ and be found in him, not having a righteousness of my own that comes from the law, but that which is through faith in Christ—the righteousness that comes from God on the basis of faith. I want to know Christ—yes, to know the power of his resurrection and participation in his sufferings…" (Philippians 3:7–11, NIV). Paul told us that whatever he had before he knew Jesus, and whatever he gained afterward, was garbage compared to the faith and grace that he gained in knowing Jesus Christ. Paul said that he would throw everything away—all of it—in a heartbeat, because knowing Jesus far surpassed any and all things that he could ever accumulate for himself here on this earth.

Tony doesn't burden himself with this world's garbage either. He's driven by a higher purpose. The love of Jesus wakes him up every morning to see who he can save. He is serving the Lord wholeheartedly as he introduces Jesus Christ and puts His word in the hands of sinners. He's "making ready the people, preparing them for the coming of the Lord!"

Tony lives on the streets, but he is not homeless. In fact, he has a most magnificent home being prepared for him. When you walk by the light of God, you are surely on the path that leads home. I know he'll be opening the door there, welcoming his saints.

"But if we walk in the light, as he is in the light, we have fellowship with one another, and the blood of Jesus, his Son, purifies us from all sin" (John 1:7, NIV).

If You Can?

Many of us put faith in our alarm clocks to wake us up and seldom worry that it may fail. There is little doubt that when we turn our faucet on in the morning that water will come out. We trust the navigation on our phones, using something we cannot see, to give us direction, choosing the path we believe best traveled. Yet, as believers, we still sometimes find difficulty in putting our unabashed faith in God. While we may trust our technology, we may also allow an inkling of doubt to step inside the shadow of our faith.

"Trust in the LORD with all your heart and lean not on your own understanding; in all your ways acknowledge him, and he will make your paths straight" (Proverbs 3:5–6, NIV).

James wrote, "He who doubts is like a wave of the sea, blown and tossed by the wind" (James 1:6, NIV). Still, doubt affected even the disciples. Peter struggled when Jesus called to him. "Come," he said. Then Peter got down out of the boat, walked on the water and came toward Jesus. But when he saw the wind, he was afraid and, beginning to sink, cried out, "Lord, save me!" Immediately Jesus reached out his hand and caught him. "You of little faith," he said, "why did you doubt?" (Matthew 14:29–31, NIV). Doubt is a tool designed to break our trust in God. In the toughest times of life, when the future seems stacked against us, it's easy to feel distant or even left behind. In those moments, we may question God's power and sovereignty.

In Mark, Chapter 9, Jesus finds a man talking with His disciples. The man had brought his son for Jesus to heal. The boy was demon possessed and the demon caused him to convulse terribly and often threw the boy into fire and water trying to kill him.

The man said to Jesus "If you can do any-thing, take pity on us and help us." "If you can?" said Jesus. "Everything is possible for him who believes." Immediately the father exclaimed, "I do believe, help me overcome my unbelief!" When Jesus saw that a crowd was running to the scene, he rebuked the evil spirit. "You deaf and mute spirit," he said, "I command you, come out of him and never enter him again." (Mark 9:23–25, NIV)

Adversity is when we need to put our trust in God most. There's no reason for doubt, no reason to say "If you can!" We are "justi-fied by faith" (ROM 5:1, KJV), and where there is faith, there will always be unfailing hope. "The one who is in you is greater than the one who is in the world" (1 John, 4:4 NIV). He is greater than any "impossibility" we may be facing down. God will pave a path for us to overcome! No need for your phone's navigational app.

Show me your ways, O Lord, teach me your paths; guide me in your truth and teach me, for you are God my Savior, and my hope is in you all day long. (Psalm 25:4–5, NIV)

Walk without Fear

While walking alone, that feeling of fear has come over all of us. It is that eerie feeling that someone is watching you or that someone or something is behind you. You look in all directions, but there is nothing to be seen. It's there though. You can feel it following you. Where is it? Why me? Chills shoot through your spine and down your legs. Your arms begin to tingle. There's a sense of danger as your heart beats faster. You can feel its breath on the back of your neck. You begin to run. Is it evil? Does it mean harm? You race home or into a business or a busy park. Whatever it was is gone now. Maybe it was nothing, or maybe it was something. Maybe it's best not known. Where did it go? Why did it quit its chase? In Psalm 23:4, David wrote, "Even though I walk through the valley of the shadow of death, I will fear no evil, for you are with me." Perhaps the shadow was shooed away by a greater force.

God is always watching over us. He protects those who are with Him. We don't always see the war between good and evil going on around us. We may be out walking alone, but there is still an army watching over us. "Are not all angels ministering spirits sent to serve those who will inherit salvation?" (Hebrews 1:14, NIV). They may be hidden from our view, but they're here among us. They're unafraid and always willing to deploy Godly powers to protect those who love Him.

Perhaps whatever scared us on our walk was made blind by God so it could not attack. Perhaps God revealed His gallant army to the beast, and it sounded retreat. Perhaps "those who are with us are more than those who are with them." Or those that are with us are mightier! We won't know for sure in this lifetime, but it's a good bet that, as we ran away, God stepped in front of evil and evil was sent packing.

In 2 Kings, we learn how God protects those He loves. Aram (Syria) and Israel were at war. The king of Aram often made plans with his officers that no doubt were kept in strict confidence. Israel had a secret weapon though. God's prophet, Elisha, was given every detail by God and passed it along to the king of Israel. The Israelites were always one step ahead of the Syrians, and that had to change if Syria planned to win. "Go, find out where he is," the king ordered, "so I can send men and capture him." The report came back: "He is in Dothan." Then he sent horses and chariots and a strong force there. They went by night and surrounded the city" (2 Kings 6:13–14, NIV). Elisha's servant woke up that morning and found an army outside surrounding them. Frightened, he asked Elisha, "What shall we do?" Elisha was calm and without worry!

> "Don't be afraid," the prophet answered. "Those who are with us are more than those who are with them."
> And Elisha prayed, "Open his eyes, Lord, so that he may see." Then the Lord opened the servant's eyes, and he looked and saw the hills full of horses and chariots of fire all around Elisha. (2 Kings 6:16–17, NIV)

The Syrians were preparing to attack and kill Elisha. God's overwhelming force stood ready but invisible to the Syrians. God had only opened the eyes of the servant. Elisha had a demoralizing defeat planned for his enemies.

> As the enemy came down toward him, Elisha prayed to the Lord, "Strike this army with blindness." So he struck them with blindness, as Elisha had asked.
> Elisha told them, "This is not the road and this is not the city. Follow me, and I will lead you

> to the man you are looking for." And he led them to Samaria.
>
> After they entered the city, Elisha said, "Lord, open the eyes of these men so they can see." Then the Lord opened their eyes and they looked, and there they were, inside Samaria. (2 Kings 6:18–20, NIV)

Elisha had led the Syrians right into the hands of the Israelite forces. Victory belonged to Israel again!

> When the king of Israel saw them, he asked Elisha, "Shall I kill them, my father? Shall I kill them?"
>
> "Do not kill them," he answered. "Would you kill those you have captured with your own sword or bow? Set food and water before them so that they may eat and drink and then go back to their master." So he prepared a great feast for them, and after they had finished eating and drinking, he sent them away, and they returned to their master. So the bands from Aram stopped raiding Israel's territory. (2 Kings 6:21–23, NIV)

Sometimes we can't see that we have numbers on our side or that God is willing to act on our behalf. We're no different than Elisha's servant. We need God to open our eyes. Usually, as humans, when it looks like the odds are stacked against us, or when things are about to go very bad very quickly, we are not seeing the full picture. For Christians, taking a step back and taking roll call can reveal favorable odds. We may not see our God's army and flaming chariots because he has hidden them from us. The opposing force may not see them either. Trust in God. He's there with numbers.

God is a protector. If it is His will, He is perfectly willing to come with a mighty force or work His quiet wisdom. After the birth of our Savior, an angel visited Joseph and advised him to protect the baby Jesus and His mother Mary from Herod by taking them to Egypt.

> An angel of the Lord appeared to Joseph in a dream. "Get up," he said, "take the child and his mother and escape to Egypt. Stay there until I tell you, for Herod is going to search for the child to kill him."
>
> So he got up, took the child and his mother during the night and left for Egypt, where he stayed until the death of Herod." (Matthew 2:13–15, NIV)

If you are a believer, God will wake you up at night to save you. It will be easy for you to sort friend from foe, angel from enemy. He will provide the direction to avoid harm's way.

David wrote in Psalm 37, "The salvation of the righteous comes from the Lord; he is their stronghold in time of trouble. The Lord helps them and delivers them; he delivers them from the wicked and saves them, because they take refuge in him" (Psalm 37:39–40, NIV). Take refuge in the Lord. He builds a fortress around those who love Him. He'll deliver you to safety.

We need to put our confidence in God rather than ourselves. Let the battles belong to Him. When we belong to God, we can take a deep breath and let Him set things right in His own way. Let Him lead. He can decide where victories are needed, or when to save us to fight another day. He has the perfect plan already laid out before Him. We shouldn't get in His way.

What frightens you and causes you to run away? What do you have in your life that scares the living Jesus out of you? What sends chills down your spine? What is it that you're fearful of conquering? Use your faithful resource—your relationship. Ask God to surround you with His mighty army of believers. Ask Him to reveal His great multitude of soldiers, flaming chariots, and superhero angels. He is on your side. He will turn confusion into contentment, disagreements into celebrations, and battles into victories. When God steps between us and evil, evil will cower. Those who hide in the darkness will turn tail and run! God will send the enemy home with a full belly and a healthy fear of our unseen God!

Prepare to be Judged

> ...at the name of Jesus every knee should bow, in heaven and on earth, and every tongue confess that Jesus Christ is Lord, to the glory of the Father. (Philippians 2:10–11, NIV)

If you are a Christian, your knee has already bowed and your tongue has already confessed. If you are not yet a Christian, your time will come for falling to your knees and confessing. It may come before death, but if it comes after, it will be on Judgment Day.

> For we must all appear before the judgment seat of Christ, so that each one may receive what is due for what he has done in the body, whether good or evil. (2 Corinthians 5:10, ESV)

> This will take place on the day when God will judge men's secrets through Jesus Christ, as my gospel declares. (Romans 2:16, NIV)

Paul made hearts sink low and minds fall into hopelessness with those statements. God is going to judge our secrets? This can't end well for the vast majority of us. After all, we are reminded that nothing is forgotten by God, and "the very hairs on our head are numbered" (Luke 12:7, NIV), and therefore accounted for. God knows our secrets? God knows the lies? The lust? The coveting? God knows the blasphemy and everything else? All of it?

In Romans 14:10 (NIV), Paul writes that "we will all stand before God's judgment seat." Then again, in verse 12, "each of us will give an account of himself to God." Not only does God know all of the "secrets," but we are going to have to give an account of them also? It's likely that we have kept mysteries and sins hidden from this world. In some cases, we may have even fooled this world into believing we have or haven't done something, or have been someone we really aren't. The charades, the follies, and our pretentious selves will end abruptly on Judgment Day. God knows the truth—every detail—no more charades. There will only be left an accounting of those moments, thoughts, and acts—a where, when, and why, on every one of them. This may be a good time to quit fooling ourselves. When we stand before God for judgment, we will all be reduced to beggars. What we have accomplished in this world or what we have accumulated, whether real or perceived, will be meaningless.

Even Paul knew of this day for himself. In 1 Corinthians 4:4 (NIV), he wrote, "My conscience is clear, but that does not make me innocent. It is the Lord who judges me." Then in verse five, "He will bring to light what is hidden in darkness and will expose the motives of men's hearts."

If even Paul knew that he would be judged by God and freely admitted that he was not innocent, how could a man less than an apostle even begin to believe he could pass judgment? In a word—forgiveness. For those that have bowed that knee, and have confessed with their mouth that "Jesus Christ is Lord," and have asked Him to forgive them for their sins, it is forgiveness. It's hard to imagine what forgiveness will look like on Judgment Day, but in the divine words of Hebrews 7:25 (NIV), "Therefore he is able to save completely those who come to God through him, because he lives to intercede for them." It may be a stern scolding with begging and tears like when our fathers disciplined us as a child, or it may be like being in the "fly-by lane" on an expressway with an EZ pass, or it may be Jesus saying "She is part of my flock. Let her pass." However the process, you either have the EZ pass, or you don't. It could be the difference between being given a warm embrace and a "welcome" from Jesus, or hearing the words "I never knew you" leaving His mouth. The pass can be humbling to acquire, but not difficult.

> Ask, and it shall be given you; seek, and ye shall find; knock, and it shall be opened unto you. For every one that asketh receiveth; and he that seeketh findeth; and to him that knocketh it shall be opened. (Matthew 7:7–8, KJV)

Thinking back on those words, "God will judge men's secrets through Jesus Christ," we need to contemplate less about the word *secrets*, and fixate more on the words, *through Jesus Christ*. We come to Father God through Jesus. He's the only way. Knock on His door. Fall to your knees. Account for everything done wrong. Then ask for the EZ pass. He will meet you on your day of fate, having already taken the blame.

> Therefore, my brothers, be all the more eager to make your calling and election sure. For if you do these things, you will never fall, and you will receive a rich welcome into the eternal kingdom of our Lord and Savior Jesus Christ. (2 Peter 2:10–11, NIV)

Done Deal

No matter how hard we try, oftentimes we still stumble. It could be a huge sin against God and against those we love, or it could be an entire lifetime of fault. Regardless of the size or scope, the shame of sin can crush us. We pray for strength to overcome, and we bury ourselves in God's word, and yet somehow, as if taken over by a demon, we sometimes commit the same sins over and over again. Each time we fail, we lose a little more trust in ourselves, eventually drowning in anguish and inward disgust. A lifetime of shame and epic fails, and it becomes easy to believe that we may have squandered our salvation. We begin to tell ourselves, "Jesus surely wouldn't be preparing a room for someone who has done the things that I have done," or, "how could God ever love me?" A whole cast of saints have come before us though, only one of them perfect, and the rest of them not even close. They probably asked the same questions of themselves.

Paul wrote in his first letter to Timothy, "This is a faithful saying, and worthy of all acceptation, that Christ Jesus came into the world to save sinners; of whom I am chief" (1 Timothy 1:15, KJV). And then again, Paul wrote in Romans 7:15–17 (NASB), "For what I am doing, I do not understand; for I am not practicing what I would like to do, but I am doing the very thing I hate. But if I do the very thing I do not want to do, I agree with the Law, confessing that the Law is good. So now, no longer am I the one doing it, but sin which dwells in me." We sometimes feel just as Paul described. We may fully know and understand what is right and wrong. We may have all good intentions in our heart not to do what is wrong, yet we do it anyway! Then we reset, with full intentions again. "This time I'm not going to fail. I can resist this weakness, this addiction, this sin." And then we do it again! Knowing what is right, and what we wish we could do, life becomes a tug of war between sinfulness and living to please God. With this kind of constant back and forth struggle going on, it has to be hard for God to lead us "beside quiet waters" as David wrote in verse two of Psalm 23. Perhaps though that is why he also wrote the next few words: "He restores my soul."

It's easy to say to ourselves, "Jesus surely didn't die for me, I wasn't worth it," or, "God's forgiveness doesn't cover this many sins." Really think about it though. God gave His one and only Son for us—an offering to atone for our sins. *He gave his Son.* Do you think He's going to give up on us now? Jesus has already paid the price for every sin—every single one, and all of the multitudes thereafter, from Eve eating of the forbidden tree until that white horse whose rider is named the "Word of God" returns with the armies of heaven behind Him (reference Revelation 19:11–21.) He took it all on himself, carried it to the cross, and wrote the check in pain, humiliation, blood, and death—God the Son, His perfect being, the offering for all of our sin.

"All that the father gives me will come to me, and whoever comes to me I will never drive away" (John 6:37, NIV). If you have come to Jesus, He will never drive you away. In Romans 5:8 (NIV), Paul tells us, "But God demonstrates his own love for us in this: while we were still sinners, Christ died for us." Paul didn't write "for those who do not sin." Instead, God gave him the words "while we were still sinners." Jesus dying for us on the cross blotted out all of our sin from God's sight. If we have come to Jesus, when we stand before our God, all He will see is the righteousness of Jesus. You can't squander your salvation. It's a done deal.

Life as a believer can require perseverance, stubbornness, and toughness. We will have to fight false messages from the devil. The evil one wants you to believe that you can't overcome the sin in your life. He wants you to believe the fight is useless. He wants you to believe that Jesus would not die for you, and that you have already lost; why even try anymore? The devil is a liar. A swindler. A killer. He is the slimy pit of mud and mire that David was rescued from and sang about in Psalm 40. The devil is never to be trusted. All he wants is to trap us in our own sickening slop and slowly pull us under.

Peter spoke about "suffering" through sin in this life.

> And the God of all grace, who called you to his eternal glory in Christ, after you have suffered a little while, will himself restore you and make you strong, firm and steadfast. (1 Peter 5:10, NIV)

Suffering through sin is short term. God will restore us. Restored, we win over sin, and we glorify Him when we do!

God is interested in how we seek Him, how we love Him, and how we choose to live for Him. We need to let Jesus be the "shield of our salvation" and ignore those inward thoughts that second guess His power and grace. We can't allow the devil to deceive us and harden our hearts. There is no need to fall back, no need to give up, no need to perish. Surrender. Lay all of your sins before God. Reveal every detail. He will work a good work in you. The sculptor will chisel a "you" that is free of those sinful habits and free of the idolatry that masquerades as a weakness or addiction. If you stumble again, lay it before Him again. If you stumble after that, do it again. Be persistent. Be a rock in your belief. Come to Him in faithfulness as often as it takes, no matter how much it hurts. Show God how badly you need Him and how much you love and trust Him. He'll open up the shackles and set you free.

> For the eyes of the Lord range throughout the earth to strengthen those whose hearts are fully committed to him. (2 Chronicles 16:9, NIV)

> Therefore, my beloved brothers, be steadfast, immovable, always abounding in the work of the Lord, knowing that in the Lord your labor is not in vain. (1 Corinthians 15:58, NIV)

Defeating sin is not easy. It's hard labor! But when you are fighting against sin and doing it for the God you love, it won't be in vain. The erosion of goodness and morality is most often slow, silent, and nearly invisible. The rebuild process for goodness may not be immediate either. If you stay faithful in prayer, committed in belief, and come to Him always, God will respond. His restoration will be at His pace, not yours, but it will be persistent and incredibly perfect. If you seek Him, He will seek you back! It's a done deal.

Good News or Bad News?

God gave us free will. We can choose why and what we believe. We can choose if we want to be a follower of our Lord Jesus Christ, or if we don't. It answers the question, "Which do you want—the good news or the bad news?"

The good news is that God loves us. He loves us so much that he gave the world his only Son. His son willingly died for us to purify us of our sins. On the third day he rose from the dead defeating death forever. God promises the same eternal life to all those who believe in His Son. Those who believe will join in His resurrection and live forever with God in heaven.

The vision that John was shown of heaven in Revelation 21 was almost beyond what he could describe.

> The wall was built of jasper, and the city was made of pure gold, clear as crystal. Each of the twelve foundations was a precious stone. The first was jasper, the second was sapphire, the third was agate, the fourth was emerald, the fifth was onyx, the sixth was carnelian, the seventh was chrysolite, the eighth was beryl, the ninth was topaz, the tenth was chrysoprase, the eleventh was jacinth, and the twelfth was amethyst. Each of the twelve gates was a solid pearl. The streets of the city were made of pure gold, clear as crystal.
>
> I did not see a temple there. The Lord God All-Powerful and the Lamb were its temple. And the city did not need the sun or the moon. The

glory of God was shining on it, and the Lamb was its light.

Nations will walk by the light of that city, and kings will bring their riches there. Its gates are always open during the day, and night never comes. The glorious treasures of nations will be brought into the city. But nothing unworthy will be allowed to enter. No one who is dirty-minded or who tells lies will be there. Only those whose names are written in the Lamb's book of life will be in the city. (Revelation 21:18–27, CEV)

It seems so easy for those that know Jesus. When you have given your earthly life to Him, it's almost impossible to imagine how anyone could ever live without Him. He is interwoven in every detail of our days and nights. Our yoke truly is made lighter having chosen Him to help shoulder the load. He shelters us. He gives us joy. He showers us in His love. With Him, our worries become wins. His grace intercedes and purifies us, readying us for that magnificent city of God!

Know this: Jesus only intercedes for those who willfully walk through His narrow gate. All others will be judged and found guilty, then sentenced to eternal residence in hell. Have you accepted the good news or the bad news? You either have or you have refused. There is no middle ground. Abstaining is no different than refusing. Those who refuse wallow in sin without repentance. They will be force fed the bad news. After all, if they weren't following Jesus, then who or what were they following? Not accepting the message will end in damnation—cast into the fiery lake. One can't help but wonder what that horrid place might be like—torment, agony, eternal regret, horrifying beasts, bondage, torture, witches, sorcery, burning flesh, bodily decay, wretchedness, air filled with deafening and piercing shrieks, unrelenting darkness and pain, fear, and wickedness far beyond what mere humans can conceive. Ungodly disease that is Satan's wrath will fill the bowels of every prisoner. Hope will not exist. Those who chose the bad news will be eternally enslaved without rest, serving the wicked dragon and his demon legion.

It should be an easy decision. Which will it be—the death that we have all earned or the eternal life that is the gift of God? That city with streets made of pure gold and gates of solid pearl? Or Satan's wrath and eternal pain and suffering? "Seek the Lord while he may be found; call on him while he is near" (Isaiah 55:6, NIV).

In Luke 16, we gain a glimpse of hell, but learn that a great chasm separates God's home from Hades.

> And he called out, "Father Abraham, have mercy on me, and send Lazarus to dip the end of his finger in water and cool my tongue, for I am in anguish in this flame."
>
> But Abraham said, "Child, remember that you in your lifetime received your good things, and Lazarus in like manner bad things; but now he is comforted here, and you are in anguish. And besides all this, between us and you a great chasm has been fixed, in order that those who would pass from here to you may not be able, and none may cross from there to us."
>
> And he said, "Then I beg you, father, to send him to my father's house—for I have five brothers—so that he may warn them, lest they also come into this place of torment."
>
> But Abraham said, "They have Moses and the Prophets; let them hear them."
>
> And he said, "No, father Abraham, but if someone goes to them from the dead, they will repent."
>
> He said to him, "If they do not hear Moses and the Prophets, neither will they be convinced if someone should rise from the dead." (Luke 16:24–31, ESV)

Your fate on judgment day will be final. God will not cross that chasm or change His decision. God has already sent Jesus, who rose from the dead. Jesus brought us the good news. He has given us fair warning. Did you hear? Were you convinced by His message or will you be like the man who cried out to Abraham?

Each of us are the authors of our own life story. The world around us is entering into deeper darkness, but free will allows us to choose for ourselves. Good or bad?

"Your iniquities have separated you from your God; your sins have hidden his face from you, so that he will not hear" (Isaiah 59:2, NIV). Don't let your sins hide God's face from you. In the end, the chasm will be too wide. There will be no crossing over. Quench your thirst now with the righteousness that comes from believing in the good news of Jesus Christ. His grace is abundant and extravagant! We should prepare ourselves to become part of the kingdom of God. Make the struggles for worldly things and pleasures become meaningless. Follow and lead others to the love that is in Jesus. We can deliver the good news that Jesus gave us, and the good news will deliver us. We can stand on streets of pure gold on Abraham's side of the chasm.

How beautiful on the mountains are the feet of those who bring good news, who proclaim peace, who bring good tidings, who proclaim salvation, who say to Zion, "Your God reigns!" (Isaiah 52:7, NIV)

If It's Time

Have you been crawling through barbed wire?
Are those blackened eyes behind those sunglasses?
Are the last few years a blur?
If you're working seven days a week just to afford
 that fancy house, or car, or vacation.
If you're too ashamed to tell anyone what you've
 done.
If what you drink burns all the way down, or
 the pills you swallow make you dream in
 cartoon.
If you're worried about climbing the ladder or
 what others think of you.
If you're feeling unloved, unwanted, alone.
If there's filth on your hands and in your head.
If all you can pay is the interest on the plastic.
If you're tired of wandering, lost in the wilderness.
If you have been taking, taking, taking, never
 giving.
If you've gained the world yet have nothing.
If you believe there is something more.

It's time. Change something. Change what really matters. Change what you're living for. Change what you believe in. Open your Bible. If you don't have one, Google it. Start with the book of John. Fold your hands. Close your eyes. Tell the King of kings that you are ready to make a positive change in your life. Share with Him. Tell Him about all of the wrong choices. Tell Him all of your regrets. Tell Him what you're scared of. What is the weight that is crushing you?

Say, "Jesus, I need you. Without you Lord, I have done nothing right. I've made a mess of everything. I pray that you will forgive me Lord. I'm giving you my life. Lord, move me in the right direction. Show me how to fix things. Help me change. Please Lord, help me."

> I will give you a new heart and put a new spirit in you; I will remove from you your heart of stone and give you a heart of flesh. And I will put my spirit in you and move you to follow my decrees… (Ezekiel 36:26–27, NIV)

Make a radical change. Trust God. Seek Him before all things. Accept God's testimony: "God has given us eternal life, and this life is in his Son. He who has the Son has life; he who does not have the Son of God does not have life" (1 John 5:11–12, NIV).

If you accept His testimony. If you believe that Jesus is the Son of God, and that He came to die for you on the cross, and then was raised three days later, our resurrected King, you have just changed everything! You have been made blameless by the grace of God! Jesus found you guilty and then took all of the blame on himself. You've been set free! Born again!

Jesus saves those who accept Him, those that call upon His name.

> May God himself, the God of peace, sanctify you through and through. May your whole spirit, soul and body be kept blameless at the coming of our Lord Jesus Christ. The one who calls you is faithful and he will do it. (1 Thessalonians 5:23–24, NIV)

> You give me your shield of victory, and your right hand sustains me; you stoop down to make me great. (Psalm 18:35, NIV)

If you have finally found the way.

If you are finding yourself in ever increasing prayer.

If the weight of your regret has been carried away by the strength of His grace.

If you have persevered through hardships and are now focused on His glory.

If you feel the power of the Holy Spirit filling you without limit.

If you were once barren inside but now alive.

If you have been through the worst, "but you have saved the best till now."

If you know that "He must become greater; and you must become less."

If you are urged to "make straight the way for the Lord."

If you plan to spend forever standing alongside truth.

He has given His life for yours.

He will stoop down to make you great.

Thanks be to God

No matter where you may be in the world, and no matter what the language, we exhibit gratitude best when we speak. We are taught by our parents from an early age to say "thank you." When receiving a gift or being helped, when being forgiven, or even when just completing a transaction, we thank the other party for their kindness. Sometimes though, as the giver, many of us can probably remember a time or two when we deserved to hear the words but didn't. Jesus was no different.

> And as he entered a village, he was met by ten lepers, who stood at a distance and lifted up their voices, saying, "Jesus, Master, have mercy on us."
> When he saw them he said to them, "Go and show yourselves to the priests." And as they went they were cleansed. (Luke 17:12–14, ESV)

The unclean lepers, once outcasts, were almost instantly healed, now able to become meaningful and productive citizens. This was big. A miracle like this surely doesn't come along too often in life. This certainly warranted an expression of great gratitude, or so one would think.

> Then one of them, when he saw that he was healed, turned back, praising God with a loud voice; and he fell on his face at Jesus' feet, giving him thanks. Now he was a Samaritan.

> Then Jesus answered, "Were not ten cleansed?
> Where are the nine?" (Luke 17:15–17, ESV)

Only one gave thanks for the Messiah's amazing gift. Nine of the ten failed to say the words. There were nine mothers somewhere who must have fallen short in their teachings.

What amazing gifts has God given you? Has Jesus been working in your life? How should we give Him praise? Paul gives us simple directions about being thankful to God in many of his epistles. In 1 Thessalonians 5:16–18 (NIV), he teaches us, "Be joyful always; pray continually; give thanks in all circumstances, for this is God's will for you in Christ Jesus." In 1 Corinthians 15:57 (NIV), he directs us with, "…thanks be to God! He gives us the victory through our Lord Jesus Christ." Then in 2 Corinthians 2:14–15 (NIV), "…thanks be to God, who always leads us in triumphal procession in Christ and through us spreads everywhere the fragrance of the knowledge of him. For we are to God the aroma of Christ among those who are being saved and those who are perishing." Paul summed up the gospels with "thanks be to God for his indescribable gift!" (2 Corinthians 9:15, NIV). When we are given a wonderful gift such as eternal life through Jesus, we should always give thanks and praise Him with great exultations!

Give thanks for all things in your life from the smallest of life's needs to the sacrifice and resurrection of Jesus Christ. Give thanks to God as David described in Psalm 26, "proclaiming aloud your praise and telling of all your wonderful deeds. I love the house where you live, O Lord, the place where your glory dwells" (Psalm 26:7–8, NIV).

Being thankful for all things is not always easy. Paul spoke of being given a 'thorn of the flesh' to keep him humble. In 2 Corinthians 12:7 (NIV), Paul called this thorn "a messenger from Satan, to torment me" and pleaded with God to take it away.

God responded by saying, "My grace is sufficient for you, for my power is made perfect in weakness" (2 Corinthians 12:9, NIV). Paul found light in the darkness. Realizing he could be thankful even for what was tormenting him, even for what he could not control, and even for when he was weak, Paul wrote "I will boast all the more gladly about my weaknesses, so that Christ's power may rest on me. That is why, for Christ's sake, I delight in weaknesses, in insults, in hardships, in persecutions, in difficulties. For when I am weak, then I am strong" (2 Corinthians 12:9–10, NIV). What is your "thorn?" Is it lust? Is it gossip? Greed? Porn? Adultery? Drugs or alcohol? Whatever the thorn, it may be born of pure wickedness, or it may have been put there purposely by God Himself. Either way, if it brought you to kneel before the throne in repentance, asking God for His mercy, then it was the earthly mechanism He exploited to draw you close! Have you thanked God for it? For, as Paul said, when you are weak, then you are made strong. Obsessed by salvation, we leave our afflictions in the wake of our past. Thank God as afflictions are overcome by His magnificent glory! Saying "thank you" to The Creator, even for the weaknesses that torment you, reveals an inner humbleness to God that is "the aroma of Christ among those who are being saved." Praise Him!

Dear Heavenly Father, You are the Creator of all that exists. We cannot fathom your greatness and power. We thank you Lord for opening our hearts to feel your presence and to know your love. We thank you for our health and Your healing hands, and for Your rod and staff which keeps us from evil. We thank you for nourishing us, and sheltering us. We thank you even for the thorns in our flesh that remind us of our failures, and we thank you for your patience and forgiveness. We thank you for Your Word which is our hope of glory. Most of all Lord, we thank you for Your Son, and our Savior, Jesus Christ, who willingly gave up His life as payment for our sins. We thank you, Lord, for His resurrection and His promise of eternal life. We thank you Jesus for loving us and saving us. Father, we do not deserve Your goodness and mercy, but we know you are faithful. We pray now that you will use us to grow your kingdom. Open our eyes, Lord, so we can see and do Your will. Fill us with Your Holy Spirit that we may glorify Your name! We pray this in the powerful name of your Son Jesus. Amen.

The Secret

In the end, he often sat with folded hands. He could not speak. His mind surely told him, "There's not much left of me." You just knew the goodness in his heart though. He never wanted to be "a bother."

In those last days, nothing seemed to work like it once did. Enabling himself to sit, to take a step, or even just move, had long since left him. He could no longer form words. He could not grasp your hand. He had a brightness in his eyes though. That's what kept those around him focused. It's like he had a secret that he wanted to tell us, but he couldn't speak the words.

He mostly sat staring across the room. The blinds were kept closed in those last few weeks. I believe he was seeing a panorama that was hidden from us. In front of him lay a tall mountain at sunset—bright and gold on the west side, but green turning to blue on the other. In his eyes, the trees must've touched the sky, and the streams cut a beautiful path to the valley. I know he saw something as perfect as that.

He could fix anything. He could look at things and just know how they should work. If it was broke, he could piece it back. He could make things new again. He was unafraid walking through fires when he had to. He was content to work in the background but was always easily found right there close with quiet kindness. He was something special. I never once heard anyone speak bad about him. He was loved and respected.

It took nine years for cancer to consume him. It took him in small bites. It stripped him down to a hospital bed in his living room. It beat him down slowly until his last breathe. His wife was alongside him. The fight had been hers too. They were in it together, from start to finish—no matter the outcome. He had a secret though, a secret he could not tell us, a secret no one could take away from him. Cancer could not beat it out of him, nor anything else in this world. In fact, it may have been cancer that unknowingly gave it to him. God works like that. He's willing to use all things to create goodness in His name.

"Behold, I have refined you, but not like silver; I have tried you in the furnace of affliction. For my own sake, for my own sake, I do it" (Isaiah 48:10–11, RSV).

Through that long hard battle, I had often wondered how he had held onto that wonderful glimmer in his eyes. All of us around him never once heard him complain. Never did he say, "Why me?" Never did he tell us how sick he was or how much pain he felt. He didn't want anyone to feel sorry for him. In hindsight, I think it was the secret that sustained him. He may not have been able to speak about it, but there was no doubt. It was there—a bright gleam in his eyes.

A while after he had passed away, I was given his Bible. It had been thumbed through but was not greatly worn. Old letters and a few remnants from his life were stuffed between the pages, along with some yellowed newspaper clippings that were stowed behind the cover. The pages were crisp and still brilliantly white like new. I leafed through it searching for anything he had kept. Then I found it. His secret was laid bare there in front of me. That glimmer in his eyes—that ease in which he finished—was uncovered. I had wondered, and now the answer was right in front of me underlined in black ink. It must have been as plain to him as that mountain he had been staring at from across the living room. Left marked for all to find, were the words, "For this is the will of my Father, that every one who sees the Son and believes in him should have eternal life; and I will raise him up at the last day" (John 6:40, RSV).

It was a life giving secret. For him, it was greater than any treasure at the foot of that mountain. This was a precious gift personally promised to him by The Redeemer. It was victory even in defeat. It was something as perfect as that.

Banished

Wwe fail. We always have. From the very beginning we humans had difficulty with authority and doing what was asked of us. Eve was easily deceived by the serpent and it's all been a tsunami of sins ever since.

> "You will not surely die," the serpent said to the woman, "For God knows that when you eat of it your eyes will be opened, and you will be like God, knowing good and evil." (Genesis 3:4–5, NIV)

Hearing that, which one of us wouldn't have taken a bite? Being like God, gaining knowledge, and having our eyes opened are all powerful seductions. Go ahead and cast the first stone if you could have resisted. The serpent was a good con man, and Eve was an easy target. Almost too easy. You have to wonder if it was all a part of God's greater plan.

> And the Lord God said, "The man has now become like one of us, knowing good and evil. He must not be allowed to reach out his hand and take also from the tree of life and eat, and live forever." (Genesis 3:22, NIV)

With those words God "banished" man from the Garden of Eden, forever sentenced to fend for himself. Saying, "Through painful toil" and "by the sweat of your brow, you will eat your own food, until you return to the ground" (Genesis 3:17–19, NIV). God made us responsible for ourselves. No more easy living in the Garden. Man was suddenly naked, hungry, and without shelter. Man had to learn to forage and grow food. Even worse than that, man suddenly lived a life that would end in death. Having been driven out, man was being shown some tough love from the Father.

Banished forever. Forced into the wilderness. Searching for or growing their own existence. Finding shelter wherever and however they could. Living with and against the beasts. Tiresome work and worry. All of this, ending in death. It sounds like a punishment too severe.

Our God wanted man to live with Him eternally. Now though, man was a sinner, not holy, not righteous, and only slightly farther up the food chain than any other animal. Left to live forever, man would have been forced to do just that—live forever as a sinner. How would that have been much different than hell? If Adam and Eve had not been banished, and if they had not been left to perish in their sin, man could never have experienced everlasting life with our perfect and Holy God. Without suffering and then death, without an offering for their sin, without mercy, man could not be made perfect and righteous. There was only one way. Man could only be made perfect through a savior, a worthy sacrifice. God the Creator had a plan. God would allow us to live and die as captives of sin and of this world. And, as we did, He would search for those of us who cried out His name, for those of us who loved Him. He would remake those who longed to grow close to Him. He would use this world as the rock and chisel to sculpt them into "the temple of the living God" (2 Corinthians 6:16, ESV).

The Lord said, "I will bring that group through the fire and make them pure. I will refine them like silver and purify them like gold. They will call on my name, and I will answer them. I will say, 'These are my people,' and they will say, 'The LORD is our God'" (Zechariah 13:9, NLT).

God sent His one and only Son, Jesus Christ, to willingly and knowingly serve as the perfect offering and payment for the sins of all mankind. The Son paid the price tag on eternity for His flawed flock. Those that love God were made victorious forever! The serpent, even with all of his evil and trickery, was out smarted. Our sins were washed clean by the blood of the Most High. Although we will experience death, we will also know the resurrection. God's people will live forever with our Lord and Savior Jesus Christ!

Until that day, we have to rely on God to use His rod and staff to guide our path. We're no different than Adam and Eve. We've been given the same knowledge of good and evil, yet we are swindled again and again by the same serpent. Just like Eve, we're an easy target, selling ourselves for a bite of the forbidden. We have to put our faith in knowing that God is refining us. He's sculpting us into that beautiful work of art. His perfect hands will complete a glorious masterpiece in us. If we choose to follow Jesus and put our full faith and trust in God, we will walk in the path He makes for us. The grave will not hold us. We will rise up just as Jesus did and live forever with our Holy and Righteous God!! At that moment, God's believers will be as Jesus described in Matthew 5:14 (NLT), "You are the light of the world—like a city on a hilltop that cannot be hidden." And as God's people enter His Holy City in victory, it is "that ancient serpent, who is the devil, or Satan," (Revelation 20:2 NIV) that will be bound and thrown into the abyss, banished.

Whether by Many or by Few

General George S. Patton commanded the U.S. Seventh Army in the Mediterranean and Europe during World War II. He also led the U.S. Third Army in France and into Nazi Germany after D-Day. His brave troops played a significant role in the Allied victory in Europe. He also believed in the power of God and prayer. Famously, in horrifically cold winter weather, as the desperate and badly outnumbered 101st Airborne was locked in the Battle of the Bulge, Patton raced his Third Army to Bastogne to help fortify them. The brave Airborne Division had been surrounded for days with no relief, no supplies, no food, no air support, and very little ammunition. Patton reportedly called his chaplain for a meeting saying, "God has His part, or margin in everything. That's where prayer comes in." Patton asked his chaplain to craft a prayer "for good weather" that they may reach Bastogne in time to save their countrymen from the hands of the Germans. The chaplain wrote a prayer as instructed asking God for fair weather and requesting the soldiers "be armed with Thy power" to march in victory against the oppression of their enemies. The prayer was printed along with General Patton's own wishes for God's blessings to rest on each soldier. The prayer was distributed to every officer and soldier as they marched toward Bastogne on December 22nd, 1944. On December 23rd, completely opposite of all weather forecasts for the day, the sun shined, the temperature climbed, the fog lifted, the weather cleared, and the C-47s flew desperately needed food and ammunition to the 101st. Patton's Third Army made Bastogne for reinforcement, and the rest is history.

God definitely has "His part" in the works of the righteous. He works for the good of those who love Him, and He likes to win convincingly. He sometimes likes to win in such a surprising manner that it leaves the world with everlasting surety of His existence, strength, and sovereignty. He gives victory in ways that bind men's hearts with His own, knitting them into His great tapestry of eternal beauty and unending greatness. God works through us exactly how is needed, and to cause both us and those around us to grow in Him. His works wipe away even the faintest doubt that He is God, the only God, and He is in complete control from beginning to end.

Great victories against overwhelming odds is God's specialty. God used Gideon to deliver the Israelites from the oppressive Midianites in such a fashion. In Judges chapter seven, Gideon had gathered his men to go to battle against the Midianites. God wanted the victory to be seen not as a victory won by the might of Israel, but more importantly, as a battle won only by the might of God. He asked Gideon to sort out and send home a majority of his men, leaving just ten thousand to face the overwhelming number against them. Then, "...the Lord said to Gideon, there are still too many men. Take them down to the water, and I will sift them for you there" (Judges 7:4, NIV). Gideon was told by God to choose only the men who took a drink by kneeling down and scooping the water up into their mouths with their hand. After sorting them out in that manner, there were only 300 left to fight the entire forces against them. 300 against thousands and thousands.

God had a plan for so few to be victorious over so many. At the sound of Gideon's men blowing trumpets and breaking jars while surrounding the Midianite camp, God thrust fear and confusion into the Midianite soldiers who then turned on one another striking each other down with their swords. The others fled and were pursued by the Israelites. With so few, and with the mighty hand of God alongside them, Israel freed themselves from the oppressive. It was a victory that only God could have brought about.

God also forged another victory for Israel with just two men over the Philistines. In 1 Samuel chapter fourteen, Jonathan, with his armor-bearer beside him, bravely attacked a Philistine outpost.

> Jonathan told his armor bearer, "Come, let's go over to the garrison of these uncircum-

> cised ones. Perhaps the LORD will work for us, since nothing prevents the LORD from delivering, whether by many or by a few." (1 Samuel 14:6, ISV)

Jonathan climbed the steep ravine by hand and foot with his armor bearer behind him. Together, once they reached the top, in what is described as "the first attack," the two of them "killed some twenty men." "Then panic struck the whole army-those in the camp and field, and those in the outposts and raiding parties—and the ground shook. It was a panic sent by God" (1 Samuel 14:15, NIV).

> Then Saul and all his men assembled and went to the battle. They found the Philistines in total confusion, striking each other with their swords. (1 Samuel 14:20, NIV)

The Lord can carve victory for His righteous followers "whether by many or by few."

In another battle between the Israelites and the Philistines, God sent just one man to exhibit the strength and glory He freely gives to those who trust in Him. David was only a simple shepherd but as he had tended his flocks, he had been forced to fight many wild animals. As he visited his brothers on the frontlines of battle, he witnessed the Philistine champion Goliath calling out any Israelite willing to fight him to the death. The winner's army would claim victory but Goliath seemed invincible. David volunteered to fight the giant, saying "The Lord who delivered me from the paw of the lion and the paw of the bear will deliver me from the hand of this Philistine" (1 Samuel 17:37, NIV).

> David said to the Philistine, "You come against me with sword and spear and javelin, but I come against you in the name of the Lord Almighty, the God of the armies of Israel, whom you have defied. This day the Lord will hand you

over to me, and I'll strike you down… All those gathered here will know that it is not by sword or spear that the Lord saves; for the battle is the Lord's, and he will give all of you into our hands."

As the Philistine moved closer to attack him, David ran quickly toward the battle line to meet him. Reaching into his bag and taking out a stone, he slung it and struck the Philistine on the forehead, and he fell facedown on the ground.

So, David triumphed over the Philistine with a sling and a stone; without a sword in his hand he struck down the Philistine and killed him. (1 Samuel 17:45–50, NIV)

God used just one man, with no fashioned weapon, to earn victory for His people—a convincing triumph eternally woven into the history of this world.

Our Savior Jesus Christ single heartedly won a convincing and eternal victory over the evil principalities of this world too. Jesus "put aside the deeds of darkness and put on the armor of light" (Romans 13:12, NIV). Forever He strengthens His followers for battle and leads the righteous in the ongoing struggles against sin. Jesus took all of the sins of those who love him to the cross. There, He willingly laid down His life as the offering for those sins. His death did not spell victory for evil though. Instead, three days later, he arose from the grave and defeated death forever—Our Risen King! With His resurrection, Jesus defeated all evil. Oh sure, evil still dwells among us in futile despair. In the end though, Jesus will return triumphantly and forever conquer what is of this world with His great army of many! For His followers, there is life forever in the resurrected Jesus, the King of kings, and Lord of lords!

What battle are you fighting? Whatever it may be, fight it for the glory of God. Pour out your life and blood in the name of our marvelous God, and your victory will be great and overwhelming! Those around you will take notice. There will be no doubt that God is with you. He will make it obvious. They'll see that you are a freedom fighter armed by the Most High—God's warrior to lead others out of the darkness and into His immersing light. Boldly ask Him to choose you for a convincing and overwhelming victory in His name! Ask Him for His amazing power and love that you might transform others. The result may be you climbing to the top of a steep and rocky ravine by hand and foot, knowing with absolute certainty that you are the instrument that will lead to decisive victories for God, whether by many or by few.

In Your Midst

As Joshua was about to lead the Israelites into the land God had promised them, God commanded Joshua, "Be strong and courageous. Do not be terrified; do not be discouraged, for the Lord your God will be with you wherever you go" (Joshua 1:9, NIV). God often reminds us that we need not be afraid. If you praise His name, and follow Jesus Christ, then he stands ready at your side.

Using Nathan as His messenger, God spoke to King David in 1 Chronicles 17:8 (NIV), promising him, "I have been with you wherever you have gone, and I have cut off all of your enemies from before you. Now I will make your name like the names of the greatest men of the earth." Then, in addition, even as he was viciously persecuted for prophesying the word of the Lord, Jeremiah proclaimed, "But the Lord is with me like a mighty warrior; so my persecutors will stumble and not prevail. They will fail and be thoroughly disgraced; their dishonor will never be forgotten" (Jeremiah 20:11, NIV). God is never far away. Our Creator is over all, through all, and in all. He is with us in our triumphant joy and beside us when we are humbled. He lights the way when we are in the darkest of pits, and He is "the glorious riches of this mystery, which is Christ in you, the hope of glory" (Colossians 1:27, NIV).

There are moments in this earthly life when all seems lost. There are hours of tragedy, days of discouragement, and sometimes even years of groping through iniquities. When we are in a deep pit of despair, surrounded by snakes, vermin, and demons, He is with us. When we are so afraid of what evil is doing to us, and we are suffocated by darkness, He is with us. When it's hard to recall when the light last shined on your face, or when you last caught a glimpse of what was right, He is with you. The only one we can truly count on is God. Every second of every day, He will stand beside us. He hears our crying whispers and our pleading shouts. We can take rest in the arms of the Most Powerful. He will not leave us. The snakes and demons do not scare Him.

In 2 Thessalonians chapter three (NIV), Paul tells us, "…the Lord is faithful, and he will strengthen and protect you from the evil one." Paul noted that we need to pray "that the message of the Lord may spread rapidly and be honored" and that we should pray to "be delivered from wicked and evil men, for not everyone has faith." In verse five, Paul says, "May the Lord direct your hearts into God's love and Christ's perseverance." Honoring God with our constant and faithful prayer is the trigger that directs our hearts into God's love. It empowers us to persevere over the darkness and through the storms. He hears our words and knows our hearts through prayer. It is our causeway to God. Prayers are the building blocks of faith. They summon the Holy Spirit.

When Jesus calmed the storm, He rebuked the wind and rain and their fury quieted. Jesus then asked His disciples, "Where is your faith?" (Luke 8:24–25, NIV). Undoubting and unwavering faith is fearless. It "crowns us with His love and compassion." It serves as proof that Christ is in us, our hope of glory! Jesus also said in John 8:12 (NIV), "Whoever follows me will never walk in darkness, but will have the light of life." When you follow Jesus, He will "watch over your life" and give you peace—His power to overcome. You will have a constant defender by your side forever. He will be that inner voice saying, "You can do this." Allow Him to guide you and He will lead you to the throne of righteousness!

From the first page to the last, the Bible exhibits God's hope for us and His plan to lavish us with His glorious love. He speaks of being in us, making us sons and daughters, and leveling our paths. Zephaniah said it best as he described how God rejoiced as Israel was restored to Him.

> The Lord your God is in your midst, a
> mighty one who will save; he will rejoice over you
> with gladness; he will quiet you by his love; he

will exult over you with loud singing. (Zephaniah 3:17, ESV)

God rejoices even today over each of us coming to Him. God is in your midst and He is mighty! He celebrates us. He comforts us and gives us peace from the storms. Our faith in Him is cause for exultation!

Life can be a treacherous journey. With God at your side, the aftermath will be that of conquering demons, embarking on new possibilities, and celebrating God's gift of strength.

> …those who hope in the Lord will renew their strength. They will soar on wings like eagles; they will run and not grow weary, they will walk and not be faint. (Isaiah 40:31, NIV)

> …And surely I am with you always, to the very end of the age. (Matthew 28:20, NIV)

There is resilience found in walking with God, a quiet confidence that is inwardly powerful and outwardly visible. Do all things through Him who strengthens you. His light shines in your midst.

Airplane Mode

I'm old school. I don't have the Bible on my phone, my tablet, or my laptop. I just carry the book. For the most part, where I go, it goes. Whenever I have a spare moment, I use it to grow closer.

Another admission of guilt: I'm not the great conversationalist. Due to this fact, I don't necessarily enjoy airline flights. Flights force you to be somewhat social with complete strangers. I'm much more comfortable shutting off the cellphone (shutting it off is still my version of "airplane mode") and peacefully reading. My book of choice, no matter where I'm at, is my non-electronic Bible. It's not that I dislike company, but I'd rather read then make small talk with a stranger. It's one of my many flaws. However, on flights, I have found that my Bible is also a fantastic conversation starter. I carry it on in plain view. It's a powerful tool. When you open your Bible in front of strangers, it more or less says, "Beyond saying hello, let's talk about something meaningful." Nearly every flight, after the passenger beside me notices what I'm reading, they will quietly ask, "Are you a minister?" Continuing to flip through pages, my response is always the same: "Nope, just a sinner." At that very moment, they are trapped, forced to sit alongside a possible "religious lunatic!" A hand covers their mouth and a look of bewilderment wrinkles their brow. It's decision time.

They will react in one of four possible ways:

1. If they are a Christian, they open up and share their faith walk. This is my favorite. Fellowship is nourishing spiritual food. It's good to hear how others conquered demons, or overcome adversity, or how their mother demanded their butt be in the pew regardless of how badly their head hurt from the night before. Some will share extraordinary stories

of miracles that brought them to Jesus, while others grew up as a believer and always knew the peace found in being a member of the kingdom of God. Almost always too, it allows me to meet others who suffer from the same thorns that God has given me. Knowing that other Christians have to fight temptations too, inspires us to forgive ourselves and continue the good fight. It's also an opportunity to be completely transparent. "Therefore confess your sins to each other so that you may be healed" (James 5:16, NIV). There's no harm. "For all have sinned and fall short of the glory of God" (Romans 3:23, NIV). You can give them complete disclosure. You'll probably never see them again this side of heaven! Pour out everything your conscience is burdened with! That Christian beside you will be dressed in white the next time you meet.

2. Some clam up and elect to ignore the Christian zealot beside them. They close their eyes and pretend to settle in for a nap, or they fumble through the seat pocket in front of them to pull the airline magazine up in front of their faces. Their actions say, "I'm not with that Christian." In their minds, I am embarrassing myself, and therefore, it's best that they treat me as if I'm invisible. My seed has fallen along the path only to be carried away by Satan (reference Mark 4:1–20). "To whom can I speak and give warning? Who will listen to me? Their ears are closed so they cannot hear. The word of the Lord is offensive to them; they find no pleasure in it. But I am full of the wrath of the Lord, and I cannot hold it in" (Jeremiah 6:10–11, NIV). I will still give my row buddy a glimpse of what it looks like to be a Christian. Setting the example is a hit-and-run tactic, and it's always entertaining for me like giving the devil a "wet willy." Jesus gave His life as payment for my sins. He wants me alongside of Him in Heaven. He loves me enough to die for me. I'm never going to apologize for accepting Jesus Christ. I'm not embarrassed. I'm humbled. I'm thankful. I pray someday the passenger beside me will find Him too. Perhaps seeing my example of unabashed faith may help them someday receive the grace

and love that is found in Jesus Christ. Perhaps then, they will never again deny Him! "Now I want you to know, brothers and sisters, that what has happened to me has actually advanced the gospel" (Philippians 1:12, CSB).

3. Some will scan every row for an empty seat. They will quickly decide that the seat next to that pale person that is coughing and sneezing is a better spot. They'll ask the flight attendant if they can move "closer to their carry-on bag." They rejoice when the attendant responds, "Everyone is aboard, so sure." At this, the rebel in me says "adios." Again, my words have fallen on the path and were devoured. "If anyone does not welcome you or listen to your words, shake the dust off your feet when you leave" (Matthew 10:14, CSB). Metaphorically, I brush the dirt off my feet and live to witness on another flight. I consider it persecution. Jesus said, "'no servant is greater than his master.' If they persecuted me, they will persecute you also. If they obeyed my teaching, they will obey yours also. They will treat you this way because of my name, for they do not know the One who sent me" (John 15:20–22, NIV). Jesus also said in Matthew 5:10, "Blessed are those who are persecuted because of righteousness, for theirs is the kingdom of heaven." I'll collect my blessing and invest in quiet time.

4. Once in a while though, the Holy Spirit will nudge that passenger to ask, "What is the Bible really about?" Or "What do you believe?" At that moment, you know, beyond any doubt, that God is at work. He's busy pre-scheduling first-class trips to the Promised Land. God has given their attention to me, and He has also given me the words! This is a gimme. "This book is about the God that created us and all that followed. He is the one true God. He created the universe. He put the sun in the sky and he put the planets into place. He created night and day, light and darkness, land and sea, time and gravity. He made man in His own likeness, and he created a kingdom called heaven where He wants us to come join Him in everlasting life! He loves us;

that includes both you and me. After God created man, it didn't take us long to make big mistakes with our lives…things like lies, immorality, gossip, hate, stealing, lust, idolatry, and murder. These are called sins and God despises them. The "Good News" is that He knows we're going to sin. It's impossible for us not to, but He still forgives us. He sent his only Son, Jesus, to pay the price for our sins. In this book, you'll read how Jesus willingly died for the sins that you and I committed. He paid the price so you and I wouldn't have to. When you read it, you'll learn how you're not expected to be perfect. You're just expected to believe in the Son, His crucifixion, and His resurrection. His Holy Spirit will take care of the rest. In this world, we are broken and utterly worthless. With Jesus though, we are perfect and absolutely beautiful in God's eyes. The words in this book offer eternal life, an everlasting celebration with the Creator. This book will fill you with hope and courage. Frankly, once you read this, nothing can stop you. You can be fearless forever. You can be reckless in speaking His name. Oh…eventually in this world, you are going to die, but that's just the beginning. You will be raised up into God's wonderful kingdom, and you will live forever! That's what it's about, and I hope and pray that you will read it and come to believe it. It will change your life."

I believe that God purposely puts us in places to make His introduction. We can go into airplane mode anytime we want just by shutting off this world, and turning on the light of the Risen Lord!

Enter into this world everyday with the hard-bound book in your hand and in your heart. Use the words inside to inspire hope and share your faith. Be a lamp on a stand!

"For whatever is hidden is meant to be disclosed, and whatever is concealed is meant to be brought out into the open. If anyone has ears to hear, let him hear." (Mark 4:22–23, NIV)

You can be Certain

The definition of certainty is "with firm conviction that a fact is absolutely true." Even as a Christian, we can be tested occasionally on just how certain we are that we will receive eternal life with our Savior after we pass from this world. For those that are not followers of Jesus Christ, it surely seems farfetched and perhaps a bit naive. Those same feelings can drive believers to question if we are truly sure. It's not unfathomable to be 100 percent sure that Jesus, the Son of God, came to teach us and to take our sins upon Himself and then knowingly die on the cross as an offering for those sins. We can also believe, that after three days, God raised Jesus from His grave to reign over this universe forever and ever. Yet we still may have trouble believing that God will do the same for us!

There are so very few certainties in this world and that may be why it is so difficult for us to decide what is certain and what is not. We know that the sun will set in the west tonight and it will come up again tomorrow, the ocean will be salty, Kraft will make mayonnaise next week, there will be another season of the Simpson's, and McDonald's will have our McMuffins and coffee in the morning. We can probably even think of a few more. Past the surety of those things, this world is filled with very little that is definite and there lies the test of knowing beyond all doubt if God will do for us what he did for His only begotten son.

Uncertainty engulfs our daily lives, but that doesn't mean that God deals with the same. The Creator of the heavens and the earth—He who separated the light from the darkness—the Sovereign God that sifted through each of us to choose who He would grant mercy to and whose heart he would harden, seemingly would only deal in certainty. The apostle Peter wrote of the trust that can be placed in the scriptures, "no prophecy of Scripture came about by the prophets own interpretation. For prophecy never had its origins in the will of man, but men spoke from God as they were carried along by the Holy Spirit" (2 Peter 1:20–21, NIV). Hebrews chapter six reads, "It is impossible for God to lie" and we can "take hold of the hope offered to us" (Hebrews 6:18, NIV). God works in absolute certainties, and His words can be trusted with absolute surety.

Knowing this, God spoke through the apostle Paul so eloquently in Romans 6:3–6 (NIV),

> All of us who were baptized into Christ Jesus were baptized into his death…buried with him through baptism into death in order that, just as Christ was raised from the dead through the glory of the Father, we too may live a new life. If we have been united with him like this in his death, we will certainly also be united with him in his resurrection.

Then in verses eight and nine, "Now if we died with Christ, we believe that we will also live with him. For we know that since Christ was raised from the dead, he cannot die again; death no longer has mastery over him." Then in Romans 8:11 (NIV), "If the Spirit of him who raised Jesus from the dead is living in you, he who raised Christ from the dead will also give life to your mortal bodies through his Spirit, who lives in you."

Jesus often spoke about the resurrection of believers. "No one can come to me unless the Father who sent me draws him, and I will raise him up at the last day" (John 6:44, NIV). Then also, Jesus said, "Because I live, you also will live" (John 14:19, NIV). And again, "My sheep listen to my voice; I know them, and they follow me. I give them eternal life, and they shall never perish; no one can snatch them out of my hand" (John 10:27–28, NIV).

We wouldn't have to put our full faith in the written word though. The miracles of Jesus Christ were witnessed by many. Jesus was not the first to be resurrected. When Jairus had just been informed that his twelve-year-old daughter had died, Jesus instructed Jairus, "Don't be afraid; just believe" (Mark 5:36, NIV). Jesus was brought to the child's side and took her by the hand, saying, "Little girl, I say to you, get up!" Immediately the girl stood up and walked around" (Mark 5:41–42, NIV). And also, as Mary and Martha had sent word to Jesus that his friend Lazarus was gravely sick, Jesus immediately left to travel back to Bethany to be at his friend's side. Upon his arrival, Jesus learned that Lazarus had been dead for four days and he wept as Mary led him to the tomb. "Take away the stone," he said. He went on, "Did I not tell you that if you believed, you would see the glory of God?" In a loud voice, Jesus called out, "Lazarus, come out!" The dead man came out, his hands and feet wrapped with strips of linen, and a cloth around his face" (John 11:43–44, NIV).

As Paul said, we were baptized into Jesus, we became a part of Jesus, and Jesus became a part of us. With that baptism, we were also crucified with Jesus and our sins died with Jesus. It's not hard to believe that since we were baptized into the crucifixion, we were also baptized into the resurrection. The words are true. God does not lie. The scriptures are ironclad and the miracles performed by Jesus are proof of the power to resurrect life. God created life out of dust. He surely chooses when to stop and restart life. Jesus told us, "I am preparing a room for you" (John 14:2, KJV). If you have read to this point, you have not fallen back and you have not rejected Jesus. Thusly, you have booked your reservation! You can be certain of it.

Run from Evil!

Be self-controlled and alert. Your enemy the devil prowls around like a roaring lion looking for someone to devour. (1 Peter 5:8, NIV)

That devil, that deceiver, that evil one knows every trick in the book. In fact, he wrote the book—the book that leads to everlasting death. He sets traps, dangling the very prizes that he knows intrigue us most. He plots seductions and hides snares then attacks and devours us. He counterfeits success and love and then searches for those who have an appetite. He feeds our arrogance and pride with wishful pleasures, fame, and wealth. He knows what is sweet to our taste and beautiful to our eyes. "Just one more step and it can be yours."

It may look like a downhill path—smooth sailing all the way to easy street. The way toward fame and riches is heavily traveled and exciting. Eventually though, you reach the end of the road. When everything goes dark and you take that last gasp of oxygen, what then? When it's too late, what next? There will be no mulligans. "For the wages of sin is death, but the gift of God is eternal life in Christ Jesus our Lord" (Romans 6:23, NIV).

God has given us all of the tools to resist evil. He's given us our armor, our shield, our breastplate, and the sword of the Spirit. He's left it up to us. We can be weak and let Satan devour us. Or we can "be strong in the Lord and in his mighty power" (Ephesians 6:10, NIV). We get to choose. Stand "with your feet fitted with the readiness that comes from the gospel of peace" or succumb eternally to Satan?

Even Jesus was tempted. The devil offered him "all the kingdoms of the world," saying to Jesus, "So if you worship me, it will all be yours" (reference Luke 4:1–13 NIV). Jesus stood firm; confidently beating down the serpent's offers with the sword of the Spirit, the Word of God. We can do the same. We have to. We face the same evil every day. The same temptations are waved before our eyes. The devil places sultry pleasures at our grasp for immediate gratification and consumption. Satan's "feel-good" promises and illusions lure us. "If you worship me, it will all be yours." He'll give you what you long for…but at what cost?

> But mark this: There will be terrible times in the last days. People will be lovers of themselves, lovers of money, boastful, proud, abusive, disobedient to their parents, ungrateful, unholy, without love, unforgiving, slanderous, without self-control, brutal, not lovers of the good, treacherous, rash, conceited, lovers of pleasure rather than lovers of God—having a form of Godliness but denying its power. Have nothing to do with them. (2 Timothy 3:1–5, NIV)

Paul gave Timothy exceptionally good advice. When overrun with this kind of evil, "have nothing to do with them."

God Himself also gave us good insight on how best to avoid evil. He locked it out. After God had seen the wickedness of man and how "every inclination of the thoughts of his heart was only evil all the time" (Genesis 6:5, NIV), He asked Noah to build an ark for his family, and every kind of bird, and every kind of animal, and every kind of creature so they may survive the worldwide flood that God had planned. God was starting over. It was time to wash away the evil and corruption of man from the world. Once the ark had been built, Noah, his wife, his sons and their wives, and all of the birds, animals, and creatures entered the ark. "Then the Lord shut him in" (Genesis 7:16, NIV). God made sure that no evil went aboard with them. He shut and latched the door Himself! God personally made sure that no evil become a stowaway.

Joseph knew how to prevail against evil and sin too. After being sold by his brothers to Midianite traders, then sold again in Egypt as a slave, he was entrusted by Potiphor to mind his home, property, and everything in his possession. Potiphor's wife begged Joseph many times, asking him, "Come to bed with me!" (reference Genesis 39:1–23, NIV). On one such instance, Potiphor's wife grabbed his cloak to pull him near her. Joseph broke free and ran away, leaving his cloak behind!

The difficulty may be in identifying evil and calling it out for what it is. As Christians, we're not called to be tolerant of evil. We should publicly reject sin. The actions of Paul described in Acts 13 gives us an example of the abruptness with which we should speak out against evil. Paul and Barnabas had been asked to speak to the proconsul at Paphos. The proconsul had asked them to share the word of God with him. Also attending was Elymas the sorcerer, who was there defiantly speaking in opposition to God, trying to turn the proconsul away from following the faith. Then Paul, looking Elymas straight in the eyes, called him out, saying, "You are a child of the devil and an enemy of everything that is right! You are full of all kinds of deceit and trickery. Will you never stop perverting the right ways of the Lord? Now the hand of the Lord is against you. You are going to be blind, and for a time you will be unable to see the light of the sun" (Acts 13:10–11, NIV). Darkness came over Elymas, and "he groped about, seeking someone to lead him by the hand." When evil came against him, Paul courageously dug in his heels and came out swinging! He stood up and publicly named evil! No one had to guess if he was standing for God! In the same manner, we should call out evildoers, unbelievers, and those who refuse to accept the gospel of Jesus Christ. We should not mingle with sinners. We should speak to them about Jesus, and if they refuse to listen, run away from them. Wipe the dirt from your feet when you've reached a safe distance!

Paul wrote much about how we should conduct ourselves around evildoers. He had a clear and consistent message across his epistles which we should take wisdom from. In his letter to the church of Ephesus, Paul wrote, "Have nothing to do with the fruitless deeds of darkness, but rather expose them" (Ephesians 5:11,

NIV). With Thessalonica, Paul urged them to "avoid every kind of evil" (1 Thessalonians 5:22, NIV). To the Galatians, he wrote, "You, my brothers, were called to be free. But do not use your freedom to indulge the sinful nature; rather serve one another in love" (Galatians 5:13, NIV). Then also to Timothy, Paul wrote, "Flee the evil desires of youth, and pursue righteousness, faith, love and peace, along with those who call on the Lord out of a pure heart" (2 Timothy 2:22, NIV).

Don't give the devil a path. "Bad company corrupts good character" (1 Corinthians 15:33, NIV). Don't associate with evil. Aligning yourself with evil, doing wrong, and indulging in sinful behavior will only lead you down the same broad freeway followed by the unsaved. Evil can be penetrating. What we desire, what we see, what we think about, what we listen to, we eventually begin to believe. With repetition, sin becomes acceptable. Immersed in sin long enough, it becomes a permanent part of our life. What we do becomes habit. What we need becomes our idol. Satan plants what is fascinating, seductive, thrilling, fun, and risky as seeds of destruction to grow inside us. Once we find something that excites us, we are lured back for a second time, then a third, then a fourth, suddenly we are lost in the sin. In the end, what seemed like fun and fascination is replaced with death and torment. Satan roams the earth deceiving the weak in faith. He lures. He seduces. Then he devours.

Resist evil! Recognize the devil's temptations and run away from them! You have the strength to oppose sin! "Not by might nor by power, but by my Spirit," says the Lord Almighty" (Zechariah 4:6, NIV). Jesus willingly died for you and now He lives in you. Don't disappoint him. Replace the temptation that very instant with prayer. "Submit yourselves, then, to God. Resist the devil, and he will flee from you" (James 4:7, NIV). Submit to the Word of God. Use His Word as your weapon, your sword. "Do not set foot on the path of the wicked or walk in the way of evil men. Avoid it, do not travel on it; turn from it and go on your way" (Proverbs 4:14–15, NIV). If you live your life doing "everything that is right," turning away from "everything that is wrong," the devil will give up and move on.

Identifying what is wicked and then turning away is not easy. It won't be mainstream or popular either. Expect to be ridiculed. The vocal majority will fiercely attack your beliefs. "In fact, everyone who wants to live a Godly life in Christ Jesus will be persecuted, while evil men and impostors will go from bad to worse, deceiving and being deceived" (2 Timothy 3:12–13, NIV). Overcoming sin and temptation can be a difficult and lonely task. Don't give up. No matter how difficult, stay off that broad freeway of desire. Follow the narrow path, the path far less traveled, through the narrow gate. "But small is the gate and narrow the road that leads to life, and only a few find it" (Matthew 7:14, NIV).

In the gospel of Luke, Jesus was asked by an expert in Jewish law, "What must I do to inherit eternal life?" Jesus responded by asking the man how he interrupted the law. The man answered: "Love the Lord your God with all your heart and with all your soul and with all your strength and with all your mind" (Luke 10:25–27, NIV). That is the formula for everlasting life. That is also how you avoid evil and sin. Loving the Lord has to come before money. Loving the Lord has to come before sex. Loving the Lord comes before your work or business. Loving God comes before your social media. Loving God comes before that new car or that vacation in the islands. Loving God comes before the awesome party this weekend. Loving God comes before your family, your friends, your success, your technology, and your on-line fantasies. God has to be put before everything, even yourself. When God is always on the top of your list no matter what, you will avoid all of the devil's traps and seductions. You'll travel the narrow way through the narrow gate, and the devil will pass you by in search of easier prey. The result will be eternal life in a kingdom so amazing we cannot even begin to conceive it.

The Least of These Sheep

God had much to say to Ezekiel about sheep. God gave him prophecy—a parable about how His flock would be taken care of. In Ezekiel 34:12 (NIV), God told Ezekiel, "I will rescue them from all the places they were scattered on a day of clouds and darkness." In verse fourteen, "I will tend them in good pasture." In verse sixteen, "I will search for the lost and bring back the strays. I will bind up the injured and strengthen the weak, but the sleek and the strong I will destroy." God went on to tell Ezekiel in verse twenty-five, "I will… rid the land of wild beasts so that they may live in the desert and sleep in the forests in safety." And then in verse twenty-eight, "They will no longer be plundered by the nations, nor will animals devour them. They will live in safety, and no one will make them afraid."

"As for you, my flock, this is what the Sovereign Lord says: I will judge between one sheep and another, and between rams and goats." (Ezekiel 34:17, NIV).

It can be difficult to judge the difference between sheep and goats. There are fundamental differences though. Goats have upright horns atop their head. Sheep, for the most part, do not have horns, or their horns curl down and around the side of their heads. Goats have coats that don't require shearing, while sheep grow wool to be sheared yearly. Goats tend to be independent, strong willed, and mischievous. Sheep are more docile and tend to enjoy being together in a herd. Goats will behave as they want. Sheep will follow their shepherd.

Jesus Christ spoke of separating the sheep from the goats also. "When the Son of Man comes in his glory, and all the angels with him...he will separate the people one from another as a shepherd separates the sheep from the goats. He will put the sheep on his right and the goats on his left" (Matthew 25:31–33, NIV). Jesus then proclaimed that the sheep on the right have been blessed by the Father and will be given their inheritance in God's kingdom. "For I was hungry and you gave me something to eat, I was thirsty and you gave me something to drink, I was a stranger and you invited me in, I needed clothes and you clothed me, I was sick and you looked after me, I was in prison and you came to visit me" (Matthew 25:35–36, NIV). Not knowing exactly what He meant, the righteous then asked Jesus when they had done these things for him. Jesus replied, "I tell you the truth, whatever you did for one of the least of these brothers of mine, you did for me" (Matthew 25:40, NIV). Jesus went on to face the goats on His left and said, "Depart from me, you who are cursed, into the eternal fire prepared for the devil and his angels." They had not offered food or drink. They had not invited the stranger in. They had not provided clothes, comforted the sick, or visited those imprisoned. The goats were sent to eternal punishment, as Jesus said, "Whatever you did not do for one of the least of these, you did not do for me" (Matthew 25:45, NIV).

In Jesus's time, the disciples were sent out to spread the gospel with no guarantee of food or water, no shelter, no change of clothes, and no plan if they were hurt, sick, or imprisoned. They were dependent upon the goodness of others to assist them as they brought the word to the masses. In the eyes of new believers, they were mighty men offering the path to salvation. To the non-believers, our evangelizing brothers and sisters were often treated as much less than "one of the least of these." Today, if you are spreading the good news, like Peter, James, Andrew, Matthew, etc., then you too are "one of the least of these." If you have accepted the gospel, really accepted it, and are a follower, then you probably also talk to others about Jesus Christ. You're a sheep and part of the flock! If you thumb your nose at modern apostles, showing contempt for believers of the gospel, then whatever you do against them or say against them, you also say and do against Jesus. You are a goat. Unless you open your eyes to see, and your heart to accept, you're going to stand on Jesus's left and your eternal future doesn't look promising.

By simply believing in Jesus Christ as our savior and as the Son of God, we have received His grace and the Holy Spirit. We are being filled and refilled every day. What we have done for "one of least of these" will not decide our salvation or if we truly are sheep. We are chosen and forgiven by the grace found only in Jesus. However, as believers, having been led by the Holy Spirit and the teachings of Jesus, we will be easily identified as His sheep and set aside from the goats by our goodness. The sheep will have invited in, fed, sheltered, and comforted, "the least of these brothers and sisters." The goats will have shown persecution and mistreatment toward God by refusing to hear His word and accept the Son. Like the sheep, the goats will be identified by their actions toward "the least of these brothers and sisters."

As sheep, we will follow the direction given by the shepherd. In Hebrews chapter 13 (NIV), we are told, "Continue in brotherly love. Do not neglect to show hospitality to strangers, for by so doing some people have entertained angels without knowing it…" and "Do not neglect to do good and to share what you have, for such sacrifices are pleasing to God." 1 John 4:20 (NIV) reads, "If someone says, "I love God," and hates his brother, he is a liar; for the one who does not love his brother whom he has seen, cannot love God whom he has not seen." Then in 1 John 4:21 (NIV), we are commanded, "And he has given us this command: Anyone who loves God must also love their brother and sister."

As God told Ezekiel, He had plans for His flock of sheep. He wanted them taken care of. He wanted to provide for their every need until Jesus separated them from the blasphemers, persecutors, haters, and evildoers. Then, on that day, they would triumph over the goats and rams and receive their eternal inheritance into the kingdom of Heaven!

Revelation chapter seven tells us how a great multitude of these sheep will stand before the throne and the Lamb—their coats made white. John was told, "These are they who have come out of the great tribulation; they have washed their robes and made them white with the blood of the Lamb" (Revelation 7:14, NIV). When these sheep receive their blessings, there will be no more suffering, no more shame, no more needs, no more sin. The "least of these" will be made blameless in Jesus Christ who will provide a perfect eternal life.

"He who sits on the throne will spread his tent over them" (Revelation 7:15, NIV). To the "least of these," Jesus will "invite them in."

"Never again will they hunger; never again will they thirst" (Revelation 7:16, NIV). To the "least of these," Jesus will give food to the hungry, and drink to the thirsty.

"The sun will not beat upon them, nor any scorching heat" (Revelation 7:16, NIV). To the "least of these," Jesus will cover and shelter them.

"For the Lamb at the center of the throne will be their shepherd; he will lead them to springs of living water. And God will wipe away every tear from their eyes" (Revelation 7:17, NIV). To the "least of these," Jesus will give eternal life, wellness, and comfort.

When asked which of the commandments were most important, Jesus responded, "Love the Lord your God with all your heart and with all your soul and with all your mind and with all your strength. The second is this: 'Love your neighbor as yourself.' There is no commandment greater than these" (Mark 12:30–31, NIV).

With these two commandments, the Shepherd will separate the sheep from the goats.

His Called, His Chosen, and His Faithful

> They will make war against the Lamb, but the Lamb will overcome them because he is Lord of lords and King of kings—and with him will be his called, chosen, and faithful followers. (Revelation 17:14, NIV)

Already loving Jesus, and already saved by grace alone, as Christians, we are hopeful of being "chosen." Being saved by the blood of Jesus Christ sets us apart. Should we rest in His arms now though? We could if we wanted. We have been invited into the kingdom. Is there possibly more though? How do we also earn the title of "faithful follower?"

In the parable of the wedding banquet, Matthew 22:1–14 (NIV), Jesus explained that, "The kingdom of heaven was like a king who prepared a wedding banquet for his son. He sent his servants to those who had been invited to the banquet to tell them to come, but they refused to come." Then the king sent more servants and asked them to come again, but they worked in their fields or at their businesses instead. Some even seized the king's servants and killed them! Outraged, the king sent his army and "destroyed those murderers and burned their city." With the wedding banquet and food being ready, the king, yet again, sent his servants to seek out guests. This time, he instructed them to gather anyone they could find, regardless if they were good or bad, and fill the banquet hall. "But when the king came in to see the guests, he noticed a man there who was not wearing wedding clothes. 'Friend,' he asked, 'how did you get in here without wedding clothes?' The man was speechless. Then the king told the attendants, 'Tie him hand and foot, and throw him outside, into the darkness, where there will be weeping and gnashing of teeth.' Jesus finished by saying, "'For many are invited, but few are chosen.'"

If God has made Himself known to us, we can send in our RSVP. We are welcome to celebrate at the banquet! Yet some of us are invited and still turn down the offer. Some of us may just be too busy "tending our own fields" or "managing our own business," to take time to attend. Some of us may consider attending but then think it may not be worth the bother or maybe putting on our "wedding clothes" just seems like too much trouble. Some of us may not even open the invitation. The parable speaks of those who have been invited, or called. Jesus says though that few are "chosen."

In Romans 1, Paul is clear that we have all been 'called.'

> The truth about God is known to them instinctively. God has put this knowledge in their hearts. From the time the world was created, people have seen the earth and sky and all that God made. They can clearly see his invisible qualities—his eternal power and divine nature. So they have no excuse whatsoever for not knowing God. (Romans 1:19–20, NLT)

So how do we become 'chosen?' Elijah was told in 1 Kings 19 by God that anyone that "worships or bows to another God" (Baal) would not be chosen. The wedding parable suggests that we should not be consumed by our worldly ambitions. Many scriptures instruct us to free ourselves of sexual immorality, resist gossip, honor our parents, stay faithful in marriage, love our neighbors, show mercy and forgiveness, etc. Even when we falter, and all of us do, grace covers every last one of those that are chosen. If we want to be "faithful followers" however, believing that Jesus, the Son of God, whom gave His life as ransom for ours, is just the beginning of the transformation. To be chosen and a faithful follower, we will need to walk in the same path as The Redeemer, and live not as this world would judge as righteous but, instead, as God urges:

> For this very reason, make every effort to add to your faith goodness; and to goodness, knowledge; and to knowledge, self-control; and to self-control, perseverance; and to perseverance, godliness; and to godliness, mutual affection; and to mutual affection, love. For if you possess these qualities in increasing measure, they will keep you from being ineffective and unproductive in your knowledge of our Lord Jesus Christ. (2 Peter 1:5–8, NIV)

We'll need to craft each day as a tribute to God, as a fragrant offering, and then give all of the glory to Him. Living our faith may not always align with what seems right to others and that may just be what separates those who celebrate with the Groom and His bride, from those who are tied up and thrown into the darkness.

As believers, we are also reminded that what this world deems as success, has little to do with being chosen and receiving our inheritance from God.

> Listen, my dear brothers and sisters: Has not God chosen those who are poor in the eyes of the world to be rich in faith and to inherit the kingdom he promised those who love him? (James 2:5, NIV)

It's your choice, but if God has called you, or invited you, make sure to accept. The chosen will answer Him quickly, and they will wear the proper wedding clothes. The faithful, knowing full well that "while we were still sinners, Christ died for us" will honor Him with their actions and with their lives. They will praise Him always. They will speak his name often. They will give food to the hungry. They will give drink to the thirsty. They will visit the sick and those that are imprisoned. They will clothe those in need. They will do this for the least of our brothers and sisters, and therefore, in faithfulness to Jesus Christ.

God is sovereign, so as Christians, we are certain of the truth. Those who gain the title of "chosen" and His "faithful follower" will be those who are "called by His grace," (Galatians 1:15), and those who seek His face with unwavering trust, and those whose actions freely display the love of Jesus to others.

Celebrate!

Both here and in heaven, victories are celebrated! You may have already been a believer in our Lord and Savior Jesus Christ, or perhaps you are about to give your life to Him now! Welcome to the kingdom of God! Praise Him!

You were the lost sheep that the Shepherd left the flock in search of. The Shepherd found you and joyfully scooped you up. He put you on His shoulders and carried you home. He called out to His friends and neighbors, "Rejoice with me; I have found my lost sheep" (Luke 15:6, NIV). Jesus said, "There will be more rejoicing in heaven over one sinner who repents than over ninety-nine righteous persons who do not need to repent" (Luke 15:7, NIV).

You were the lost son who returned home to the Father. "While he was still a long way off, his father saw him and was filled with compassion for him; he ran to his son, threw his arms around him and kissed him" (Luke 15:20, NIV). They quickly prepared a feast. They put a ring on his finger. They celebrated his return! "For this son of mine was dead and is alive again; he was lost and is found. So they began to celebrate" (Luke 15:24, NIV).

You were the lost coin that Jesus spoke about as He described a woman frantically searching by lamp light. When it was found, she called her friends and family together and said, "Rejoice with me; I have found my lost coin" (Luke 15:9, NIV). Jesus again followed with, "In the same way, I tell you, there is rejoicing in the presence of the angels of God over one sinner who repents."

When you accepted Jesus Christ into your heart, Heaven had a party in your name! The seraphim hovered and quieted their wings awaiting His words. The cherubim lowered their praise a few octaves and came to attention before the Heavenly Host. Jesus stood up from

His throne with a smile as wide and beautiful as the morning sun. His voice rang out across the halls of heaven, "Rejoice! A sinner has repented and given his life to the Father!" The music was cranked up and the angels danced until they dropped! The drums pounded. The trumpets sounded. The flutes, and lyres, and harps, backed up the Hallelujah Choir! The very armies of God had hands in the air waving back and forth, giving praise and glory to God! Twelve apostles got up from twelve thrones and did a touchdown dance in unison! Then, for a few brief minutes, Gabriel called for silence, and there was silence, while Elvis sang "Amazing Grace." Brother, your victory was celebrated!!

David wrote in his Psalm of Thanks what the result is when we "ascribe to the Lord the glory due his name." "Let the heavens rejoice, let the earth be glad; let them say among the nations, "The Lord Reigns!" (1 Chronicles 16:31, NIV). David continued with worship for our Lord "in the splendor of his holiness." "Let the sea resound, and all that is in it; let the fields be jubilant, and everything in them! Then the trees of the forest will sing, they will sing for joy before the Lord..." (1 Chronicles 16:32–33, NIV). No celebration compares to that which takes place when a sinner comes to the cross and surrenders their life to God. Nothing glorifies God more than when we say, "I can't do this on my own. I beg of you Father, I want to be with you forever. I pray you will forgive me! Please Lord, find me right here where I stand. I am yours! I need Jesus!" From that moment on, the Father is filled with compassion for you. He runs to you. He throws His arms around you and kisses you! You are filled with the warmth, comfort, and confidence that only God can give His people in such abundance. Brokenness is made whole and fear is replaced with courage. The Holy Spirit goes where you go. He is with you! You are reborn!

Therefore, if anyone is in Christ, the new creation has come: The old has gone, the new is here! (2 Corinthians 5:17, NIV)

His sun dries the dew from the leaves. Melting snow streams from the mountaintops. His flowers open petals in first bloom. New life engulfs you. The old is dead and buried. The new will live forever! The angels have placed a seat for you at the banquet table! Celebrate!

Who Was Barabbas?

It was a raucous crowd with shouting, pushing, and shoving. Emotions were raw for most. There were high ranking officials, high priests, and Jews of every walk of life, together, waiting for Pontius Pilate to follow custom and grant a prisoner his freedom—a free pass decided by the onlookers.

> The chief priests and the elders persuaded the crowd to ask for Barabbas and to have Jesus executed.
>
> "Which of the two do you want me to release to you?" asked the governor.
>
> "Barabbas" they answered.
>
> "What shall I do, then, with Jesus who is called Christ?" Pilate asked.
>
> They all answered, "Crucify him!"
>
> "Why? What crime has he committed?" asked Pilate.
>
> But they shouted all the louder, "Crucify him!" (Matthew 27:20–23, NIV)

Barabbas had won the lottery of sorts. Even Pilate could not seemingly justify how the crowd could plead so passionately for Barabbas's forgiveness over a man who had done nothing wrong in the eyes of Roman law. After all, "Barabbas had been thrown into prison for an insurrection in the city, and for murder" (Luke 23:19, NIV). History identified Barabbas as notorious, rebellious, a thief, and a murderer. Yet it was Barabbas that was forgiven and freed. By the crowd's actions, Jesus was sent to his crucified death in place of a sinful rebel.

You have to wonder what Barabbas was thinking. Hadn't this man named Jesus made the blind to see? Hadn't Jesus brought the dead back to life? Barabbas had to ask himself, "How could these people favor me over this perfectly innocent man?" It was certainly good fortune. A completely unexpected second chance at life granted to him. Some would look at this type of opportunity as a "new life." So did he do anything meaningful after he was forgiven? We don't know. He was not mentioned again in biblical text.

Barabbas truly did not differ much from many of us today, or even from most Christians today. We share atrocities and commit wrongs that are much the same—rebellion, drunkenness, hate, theft, deceit, lust, adultery, and, yes, murder. Yet Barabbas was forgiven, and Jesus paid the price instead with unimaginable agony, blood, and suffocation.

> With a loud cry, Jesus breathed his last. The curtain of the temple was torn in two from top to bottom. And when the centurion, who stood there in front of Jesus, heard his cry and saw how he died, he said, "Surely this man was the Son of God!" (Mark 15:38–39, NIV)

I suppose when we ask "Who was Barabbas?" Perhaps we could look closely at our own Facebook page and find him. We may find glimpses of him in our selfies, or a few comparisons in our personal testimonies. All are masking guilt of some variety.

Let's ask that question again: Did 'Barabbas' do anything meaningful after he was forgiven?

Here I Am

As the Israelites were about to cross the Jordan River into Canaan after forty years of wandering, Moses reminded them "Now choose life, so that you and your children may live, and that you may love the Lord your God, listen to his voice, and hold fast to him" (Deuteronomy 30:20, NIV). We may live in the ways of the Lord, but do we listen for His voice?

The prophet Isaiah described seeing through the temple corridors and into heaven itself, witnessing the Lord, seated on His throne, the train of His robe filling the entire floor. Seraphs were flying about, praising the name of God as their voices thundered through the temple, shaking its walls and doorways. The Lord wanted Isaiah to spread words of warning throughout His people and speak of coming captivity because of their sin. He asked for confession, repentance, and cleansing among them, and for Him to be exalted above all things. The Lord asked for a messenger. "Then I heard the voice of the Lord saying, 'Whom shall I send? And who will go for us?' 'Here am I. Send me!'" (Isaiah 6:8, NIV).

God can surprise us sometimes. He may show Himself in mighty glory and He may shake the walls and doorways to get our attention. But sometimes, He may just give a faint whisper barely audible above the "noise" we live amongst. Listen closely because it could merely be a signal from within since He lives within us. If we listen, we may be chosen as an instrument to deliver His will—to make change for His people. If He calls out to us, how do we respond?

As Moses was tending his father-in-law's flock, the angel of the Lord appeared to him from a burning bush. The Lord saw that Moses had crept closer and so He called out from the bush, "'Moses! Moses!' And Moses said, 'Here I am.'" The Lord then sent Moses to free the Israelite people from the Egyptians and Pharaoh (See Exodus Chapter 3:1–22, NIV).

When Abraham was tested by God (Genesis 22:1–19, NIV), God called out to him, "'Abraham!' 'Here I am,' he replied. Then God said, 'Take your son, Isaac, whom you love, and go to the region of Moriah. Sacrifice him there as a burnt offering on one of the mountains I will tell you about.'" Abraham set out the next morning with Isaac and two servants. After three days, Abraham saw the place that God had told him about for the offering to be made. Abraham placed the wood for the burnt offering on the back of Isaac for him to carry, and Abraham carried the fire and the knife. He asked the servants to stay as he and his son went to worship. As they walked further, Isaac asked, "'Father?' 'Yes, my son?' Abraham replied. 'The fire and the wood are here,' Isaac said, 'but where is the lamb for the burnt offering?'" Abraham answered, "God himself will provide the lamb for the burnt offering, my son." Once they reached the place, Abraham built an altar and laid wood upon the top of it. He bound his son and laid him on top of the wood. As he took the knife to give his only son as an offering, "the angel of the Lord called out to him from heaven, 'Abraham! Abraham!'" Abraham replied, "Here I am." The Lord told Abraham, "'Now I know that you fear God, because you have not withheld from me your son, your only son.' Abraham looked up and there in a thicket he saw a ram caught by its horns. He went over and took the ram and sacrificed it as a burnt offering instead of his son."

Samuel, the first son of Hannah, lying beside the ark of God, was called by the Lord (Samuel 3:1–21, NIV). After having been awoken twice, he felt that his priest, Eli, had called to him, and answered "Here I am, you called me?" Each time, Eli told Samuel that it was not him who was calling. On the third time, Eli told the boy, "Go and lie down, and if he calls you, say, 'Speak Lord, for your servant is listening." The Lord woke Samuel a fourth time, and the word of the Lord was given to him—a prophecy against the sin of Eli's sons and against Eli knowing of the sin and yet not correcting his sons.

King David wrote in Psalm 40:7–8 (NIV), "Here I am, I have come—it is written about me in the scroll. I desire to do your will, O my God; your law is within my heart." If we desire to do God's will, we need to be listening for God to call us. Shouldn't we respond as David, Samuel, Moses, Isaiah, and Abraham, did? Shouldn't we say, "I'm here Lord, for Your servant is listening?" When God nudges you to get up out of your chair and help your neighbor, say "Here I am." When God tells you to make food and take it to that family that is hurting, say "Here I am." When something deep in your heart urges you to ask the family next door to come to church, or to help build that school for those who can't, or to give far more than you can afford because God knows where it is needed worse, say "Here I am."

God may not set fire to the arborvitae outside our window, or shout our names from a tall mountain. We need to hear and recognize His voice when he calls us though. When the "I Am" wishes for us to anoint a king or to free His people from slavery or to speak of His grace to others, when God asks, "Whom shall I send? And who will go for us?" Answer as those greatest among us did: "Here I am."

By Faith

> Now Thomas (also known as Didymus), one of the Twelve, was not with the disciples when Jesus came. So the other disciples told him, "We have seen the Lord!"
>
> But he said to them, "Unless I see the nail marks in his hands and put my finger where the nails were, and put my hand into his side, I will not believe."
>
> A week later his disciples were in the house again, and Thomas was with them. Though the doors were locked, Jesus came and stood among them and said, "Peace be with you!" Then he said to Thomas, "Put your finger here; see my hands. Reach out your hand and put it into my side. Stop doubting and believe."
>
> Thomas said to him, "My Lord and my God!"
>
> Then Jesus told him, "Because you have seen me, you have believed; blessed are those who have not seen and yet have believed." (John 20:24–29, NIV)

Jesus had to prove it. He must've known that He would. Thomas was a doubter, and the idea of Jesus having been raised from the grave seemed a bit incredible, even for followers of the most miracle-laden man ever to walk the earth. It wasn't enough that Jesus had appeared before the other disciples already. Thomas had to see the proof for himself. He had to push his fingers into the nail holes, and his fist into His side where the spear had entered. Then, "because he had seen, he believed."

Having faith was easier when it was by sight. The first followers of Jesus Christ saw Him. They spoke to Him. They knew Him. His authority, and His goodness, was plain to see. When the lame were made to walk, when the deaf were made to hear, when demons were made to flee, His power was surely unmasked. Not to mention the marks of His demise-those nail holes and that gaping spear hole. It was unmistakable. Jesus had risen! Jesus was the Son of God! Seeing was believing!

For the early followers of God, it was harder. It was by faith and by faith alone. There was no living proof standing alongside them-showing them the marks from His crucifixion. Jesus wasn't walking with them yet, saying "Peace be with you." He wasn't there to ask them to throw their net on the right side of the boat, or to cook them fish when they came to shore (John chapter 21). They occasionally received the word of God personally, but often, when God spoke, it was through the words and miraculous signs performed by His prophets. The saints were believing largely blind. "Now faith is confidence in what we hope for and assurance about what we do not see. This is what the ancients were commended for" (Hebrews 11:1–2, NIV). They trusted in what they could not see. Their belief stood bravely by faith alone! To the faithless and those who worshipped idols, those devoted to God must have appeared radical and revolutionary.

A few examples worthy of being commended for:

> By faith Enoch was taken from this life, so that he did not experience death: "He could not be found, because God had taken him away." For before he was taken, he was commended as one who pleased God. And without faith it is impossible to please God, because anyone who comes to him must believe that he exists and that he rewards those who earnestly seek him. (Hebrews 11:5–6, NIV)

By faith Noah, when warned about things not yet seen, in holy fear built an ark to save his family. By his faith he condemned the world and became heir of the righteousness that is in keeping with faith. (Hebrews 11:7, NIV)

By faith Abraham, when called to go to a place he would later receive as his inheritance, obeyed and went, even though he did not know where he was going. By faith he made his home in the promised land like a stranger in a foreign country; he lived in tents, as did Isaac and Jacob, who were heirs with him of the same promise. For he was looking forward to the city with foundations, whose architect and builder is God. (Hebrews 11:8–10, NIV)

By faith Abraham, when God tested him, offered Isaac as a sacrifice. He who had embraced the promises was about to sacrifice his one and only son, even though God had said to him, "It is through Isaac that your offspring will be reckoned." Abraham reasoned that God could even raise the dead, and so in a manner of speaking he did receive Isaac back from death. (Hebrews 11:17–19, NIV)

By faith Isaac blessed Jacob and Esau in regard to their future. (Hebrews 11:20, NIV)

By faith Jacob, when he was dying, blessed each of Joseph's sons, and worshiped as he leaned on the top of his staff. (Hebrews 11:21, NIV)

By faith Joseph, when his end was near, spoke about the exodus of the Israelites from

Egypt and gave instructions concerning the burial of his bones. (Hebrews 11:22, NIV)

By faith Moses' parents hid him for three months after he was born, because they saw he was no ordinary child, and they were not afraid of the king's edict. (Hebrews 11:23, NIV)

By faith Moses, when he had grown up, refused to be known as the son of Pharaoh's daughter. He chose to be mistreated along with the people of God rather than to enjoy the fleeting pleasures of sin. He regarded disgrace for the sake of Christ as of greater value than the treasures of Egypt, because he was looking ahead to his reward. (Hebrews 11:24–26, NIV)

By faith the people passed through the Red Sea as on dry land; but when the Egyptians tried to do so, they were drowned. (Hebrews 11:29, NIV)

By faith the walls of Jericho fell, after the army had marched around them for seven days. (Hebrews 11:30, NIV)

And what more shall I say? I do not have time to tell about Gideon, Barak, Samson and Jephthah, about David and Samuel and the prophets, who through faith conquered kingdoms, administered justice, and gained what was promised; who shut the mouths of lions, quenched the fury of the flames, and escaped the edge of the sword; whose weakness was turned to strength; and who became powerful in battle and routed foreign armies. Women received back their dead, raised to life again. There were others who were tortured, refusing to be released so that they might gain an even better resurrection. Some faced jeers and flogging, and even chains and imprisonment. They were put to death by stoning; they were sawed in two; they were killed by the sword. They went about in sheepskins and goatskins, destitute, persecuted and mistreated—the world was not worthy of them. They wandered in deserts and mountains, living in caves and in holes in the ground.

These were all commended for their faith, yet none of them received what had been promised, since God had planned something better for us so that only together with us would they be made perfect. (Hebrews 11:32–40, NIV)

"Only together with us would they be made perfect." So what about "us?" What is the foundation of our faith? We certainly cannot see Jesus nor are we led by the prophets. We are led by His Holy Spirit. "Having believed, you were marked in him with a seal, the promised Holy Spirit, who is a deposit guaranteeing our inheritance until the redemption of those who are God's possession—to the praise of his glory." (Ephesians 1:12–14, NIV)

The disciples did see with their own eyes. Jesus stood before them, resurrected. They knew with all certainty. Yet, the first believers had just faith alone to fashion their lives. God somehow made His voice heard by them. They felt His breathe upon them. They followed His fiery pillar. They walked through the rivers and seas that stood still. They survived the great flood. They were both conqueror and slave.

Both ancients and disciples knew hate and persecution. Their faith was fiercely tested as they followed the Most High God. They were ridiculed. They were beaten, flogged, and caned. They were stoned, burned, and put to the sword. They were despised, imprisoned, fed to beasts, and left for dead. They were crucified.

As believers in the redemption found in Jesus Christ, we too are persecuted. We're laughed at. We are called "extremists." We are imprisoned around the world. We are considered the infidel. We are beaten and killed for our faith. Our churches and workplaces are targets for hate and murder. The main stream despises us. The riches and pleasures of this world tempt us. Our faith in our God is relentlessly tested.

It is the Holy Spirit that carries us. It is through Him that we "set our hearts on things above, where Christ is seated" (reference Colossians 3). The Holy Spirit teaches us to forgive. We find the strength to encourage each other through Him. We overcome persecutions. We drive evil away. We cast aside temptations. We share with those that are in need. We are humbled and patient. Our hands do God's work. It is by and through the Holy Spirit that Christ dwells in us. Having been given this Wonderful Counselor, we fully surrender to our Lord Jesus Christ. It is by His strength that we are held up, not ours.

In Paul's second letter to Corinth, he wrote, "We live by faith, not by sight" (2 Corinthians 5:7, NIV). We have not met Jesus in person, but we will. We haven't put our fingers in the nail holes, but we believe. Just like Abraham and Moses, we trust.

Blessed by the Holy Spirit, we are led over the narrowest of paths—the deep canyon on one side and the rocky crags along the other. It's a dangerous trail filled with depravity, deceit, fear, and death. The Spirit walks with us through the pit of venomous serpents. He pulls our legs and feet from the muck, and shields us from the fire. He is our breath when we are drowning. He lifts us when we fall. The Holy Spirit is our staff and our sword. When we are chosen, regardless of the terrain or the opposition, Jesus deliverers. "I know that you can do all things; no purpose of yours can be thwarted" (Job 42:2, NIV).

By faith, we know beyond all doubt, that when that last trumpet sounds, we will take our place beside Jesus, beside Moses, beside Elijah, beside Noah, Enoch, Abraham, Isaac, Joseph, Rahab, Peter, Mary, John, James. We will stand among all of His saints. We will line up alongside the King of kings! We are believers in our loving and loyal God by faith. In the end, that faith will make all the difference. We will be blessed as "those who have not seen and yet have believed."

Who Are The Blessed?

In Matthew 5, we hear Jesus speak to the crowd with the words we now refer to as "The Sermon on the Mount." Jesus gave all of us hope when he stated "Blessed are the poor in spirit, for theirs is the kingdom of heaven. Blessed are those who mourn, for they shall be comforted. Blessed are the meek, for they shall inherit the earth" (Matthew 5:3–5, ESV). He continued, "Blessed are you when others revile you and persecute you and utter all kinds of evil against you falsely on my account" (Matthew 5:11, ESV).

One can't help but wonder who Jesus was blessing. Who are the "poor in spirit?" Who are "the meek?" Don't we all hurt when we lose someone or something meaningful? As Christians, we've all felt the jeers and seen the eye rolls of a non-believer when they've heard of our love for God. So too we have all been humbled many times by our own personal actions and mistakes. Then, realizing our only means of being saved wasn't anything we could do on our own, we put our trust in Jesus Christ as our Savior. We gave up on our own selfish lives and agendas. We threw off the desires of this world and repented of our sins. Asking for God's forgiveness and mercy caused our knees to buckle, our heads to bow, and hearts to soften. Humbling indeed. "But God, being rich in mercy, because of the great love with which he loved us, even when we were dead in our trespasses, made us alive together with Christ—by grace you have been saved—and raised up with him…" (Ephesians 2:4–6, ESV).

If we admit it, we all have our crosses to bear, and we've all been downtrodden at some point. Our earthly sins and struggles come in many forms—health issues, financial hardships, relationship problems, addictions, greed, jealousy, immorality, deceit, pride, etc. There's no shortage of reasons why each of us cry out for Him as we fall short of His expectations. One need not flip too many channels either to find the ever-heightening persecution of Christians. In much of the world today, your life can be in the crosshairs if you exclaim aloud your love for Jesus Christ. Being a Christian ends in triumphant victory, but here, in the now, "how much we must suffer for the sake of His name" can sometimes seem brutal (reference Acts chapter 9).

Looking out over the crowd that day, Jesus was blessing every last one of us—His faithful. Jesus understood the difficulty in following Him. He knew that we would experience failures. He knew that we would mourn, that we would be beaten down. Being made blameless isn't easy. We willingly and joyfully allow ourselves to be abandoned by this world, betrayed alongside the One we love, the One that bought our pardon, and the One we are made alive in. More than anyone, Jesus understands the fire that refines us.

Even still, His sermon is filled with "good news" for His followers! He's an equal opportunity giver of grace! With Jesus by your side, you've been acquitted of every wrong. Cast aside those chains. You are freed of those burdens. No more wandering. No more self-condemnation. Live forgiven. Whatever has made life difficult for you has garnered you a blessing from Jesus Christ Himself! He knew exactly who He was talking about when He spoke that day. It was you and I! Wrap yourself in His love! Feel the warmth of His light! "Rejoice and be glad, for your reward is great in heaven…" (Matthew 5:12, ESV).

A Camel Named Rockefeller

Standard Oil Company was a behemoth. With humble beginnings as a refiner of kerosene for lamp oil, John D. Rockefeller quickly grew what would eventually control over 90 percent of all oil production and 85 percent of the final sales of related oil products in the United States. "The Standard" accomplished this by aggressively purchasing all rival oil companies, squashing start-ups, and leveraging their size to discover new economies of scale that lesser but competitive companies could not. Their size and volume allowed them to manipulate costs with railroads, and to invest in pipeline infrastructure that led to great logistical advantages. Standard Oil ruled the oil business long before the automobile. Then, as it became apparent that axles and steering wheels would replace bridals and buckboards, the value of the business become truly difficult to conceive. By 1911, citing price gouging, unfair business tactics, and monopoly strategies, the U.S. Supreme Court forced Standard Oil to be split up. Although a smaller Standard Oil would still remain, an impressive list of conglomerates were spawned as a result. Companies and brands we recognize today were formed from the bits and pieces of what was largely held by John D. Rockefeller—Esso, Vaseline, Pennzoil, Exxon-Mobil, Chevron, Unocal, Amoco, BP, and Marathon were a few of the many that we still recognize.

By 1912, John D. Rockefeller had long since been retired from active business life, and had a reported net worth of $900 million. Translated into today's monetary numbers, he would still be the richest man who has ever walked this globe, richer than many countries. At the young age of twenty-one, already in his own commodity and bookkeeping business, Rockefeller assisted his church through a financial crisis with a $2,000 gift—a sizable gift for the era. Then later in life, he and JP Morgan, pooled some of their capital and bailed out the US government from financial collapse.

Above all things, Rockefeller was a Christian. Upon gaining his first real job, he immediately began tithing 10 percent each week to his Baptist Church, which he continued throughout his entire life. He honored the Sabbath each and every week without fail, going to church and spending time with his family. He prayed daily. He also attended or hosted bible study at least one night each week.

His mother, Eliza Rockefeller, instilled her Christian faith in John early on. Growing up, she taught him to be frugal and to value a dollar. He was expected to work hard and live thrifty. He earned his own money as a boy by doing odd jobs, selling candy, and raising turkeys. Wastefulness was not tolerated by his mother, but saving and giving for the greater good was demanded.

Rockefeller made his first major business transaction at twelve years old. He loaned $50 to a farmer at 7 percent interest. After one year, his return on investment was $3.50. That same loan today would have been about $1,500, and his interest would have raked in an extra $105. It was an eye opener to young John D. He learned that having money made it easier to make more. It was a simple formula—hard work and sound logic made his bank account grow and grow and grow and grow to a level that when adjusted for inflation, no one yet has really even come close to matching.

If you had asked him, Rockefeller probably would have told you that he wasn't truly gifted in anything except the business of making money. He unknowingly had an advantage though. He knew Jesus Christ well and he trusted Him. He would have read and understood the sound investment strategy that Jesus offered. Although just casually mentioned by Jesus, the reward far outweighed the risk for those with unwavering trust. It was both lucrative and fool proof.

In Matthew 19:16–30, a young and very wealthy man had approached Jesus and asked him what he must do to gain eternal life. Jesus responded by telling him he must obey the commandments.

> "Do not murder, do not commit adultery,
> do not steal, do not give false testimony, honor

your father and mother, and love your neighbor as yourself."

"All these I have kept," the young man said, "What do I still lack?"

"Jesus answered, "If you want to be perfect, go sell your possessions and give to the poor, and you will have treasure in heaven. Then come follow me."

When the young man heard this, he went away sad, because he had great wealth.

Then Jesus said to his disciples, "I tell you the truth, it is hard for a rich man to enter the kingdom of heaven. Again I tell you, it is easier for a camel to go through the eye of a needle than for a rich man to enter the kingdom of God." (Matthew 19:19–21, NIV)

The disciples struggled with the question, if a rich man may be denied eternal life, how could they ever reach heaven? Peter, knowing that the rich young man had just been told to give up his possessions and follow Jesus, said, "We have left everything to follow you! What then will there be for us?" (Matthew 19:27, NIV). Jesus said to them, "Everyone who has left houses or brothers or sisters or father or mother or children or fields for my sake will receive a hundred times as much and will inherit eternal life" (Matthew 19:28–29, NIV).

Rockefeller may have done the math. If he did, multiplying by a hundred must have opened his eyes and his heart. While in prayer, Rockefeller said that God spoke to him, "All the money in the world will do you no good in heaven or hell, your job and your responsibility is to give it away." He took the word of his savior as gospel and went to work doing just that.

Paul's words to Timothy surely had inspired him as well.

> Command those who are rich in this present world not to be arrogant nor to put their hope in wealth, which is so uncertain, but to

put their hope in God, who richly provides us with everything for our enjoyment. Command them to do good, to be rich in good deeds, and to be generous and willing to share. In this way they will lay up treasure for themselves as a firm foundation for the coming age, so that they may take hold of the life that is truly life. (1 Timothy 6:17–19, NIV)

"Being endowed with the gift I possess, I believe it's my duty to make money and to use the money I make for the good," Rockefeller said, then he used the remaining forty years of his life to fund works for God with his vast wealth. Knowing the Creator of all things, he said, "God gave me my money." He hired Frederick Gates, a man of God, to help him set disciplines and criteria for putting his massive wealth to work for the greater good.

Gates once warned Rockefeller, saying, "Mr. Rockefeller your fortune is rolling up like an avalanche! You must distribute it faster than it grows! If you do not, it will crush you and your children and your children's children!"

The John D. Rockefeller Foundation funded many prestigious colleges including the University of Chicago and Spelman College for African American women. He financially enabled the opening of 800 high schools in the southern United States and created many medical research foundations that impacted health advancements around the world. Medical cures for meningitis, yellow fever, and hook worm were found by research bank rolled by Rockefeller. He had a passion for providing comfort, food, and healing to the sick and the poor. He generously gave to Christian missionaries around the world. He diligently opened the envelopes of those in need and spread God's love humbly and without drawing attention to himself.

In his eightieth year, Rockefeller set the philanthropic bar highest by giving $138,000,000 to charity. Rockefeller met Jesus in person in 1937 at the age of ninety-eight. When his estate was tallied up afterward, his $900,000,000 net worth in 1912, had been reduced to

$26,400,000. He had given away over 97 percent of a mind-boggling fortune diligently doing God's work.

> Calling the crowd along with his disciples, he said to them, "If anyone wants to follow after me, let him deny himself, take up his cross, and follow me. For whoever wants to save his life will lose it, but whoever loses his life because of me and the gospel will save it. For what does it benefit someone to gain the whole world and yet lose his life?" (Mark 8:34–36, CSB)

A camel through the eye of a needle? "…with God all things are possible" (Matthew 19:26, NIV). John D. Rockefeller proved it.

Sources:

http://www.giantsforgod.com/john-d-rockefeller-sr-standard-oil/
https://en.wikipedia.org/wiki/John_D._Rockefeller
https://thegooddemocrat.wordpress.com/2007/04/03/on-rockefe
    ller-being-rich-and-being-religious/
https://www.challies.com/articles/the-philanthropists-john-d-rocke
    feller/

Do Something Dangerous

The Center of Studies on New Religions released a report in early 2017 that declared the number of Christians martyred for their faith at 90,000 for 2016. Across this earth, rather than denying their love for Jesus, they chose death, the ultimate testimony to their strength of faith and trust!

> For whosoever will save his life shall lose it:
> and whosoever will lose his life for my sake shall
> find it. (Matthew 16:25, KJV)

In today's world, it's growing easier to become a martyr for Jesus Christ. It could be as easy as preaching His gospel in front of a local shopping plaza, or feeding hungry people in parts of the world that do not love Him. Speaking His word to those lost in untruth will often result in peril. If you live and share Jesus's gospel daily, like it's the reason you are breathing, evil will wield a worldly sword against you sharpened by revenge. Ready yourself! Put on your "full armor," strap on that "belt of truth," and "take up that shield of faith" because those flaming arrows may already be in flight (reference Ephesians 6:10–18).

Look behind you often! When you least expect it, evil will rush you from behind and throw you to the ground. With the wind knocked out of you, it will find a rock and violently crack your skull open. While you gasp for air, and bleed from your temple, it will pierce your back with a sharp spear and then thrust it through. The thought of it makes even the most faithful consider what their reaction might actually be if put to the real test. Deny Christ and avoid this pain? Or tell evil about God's grace the moment before you meet Jesus?

Being a martyr may not always require loss of life. It may be as simple as making a life changing decision. One can almost picture that salesperson deciding to change strategies, saying, "I'm not omitting the dirty details to close the sale anymore." In a way, it would be like saying, "I'm not denying Jesus to make quota. Instead, I'm going to live and breathe my faith no matter what it costs me." That same salesperson may even shift into missionary mode with, "I'm giving up on this comfortable salary. I'm going to do something bigger, something of far greater worth." Like a snake that sheds its skin, clarity can unveil itself. "I'm done with this crazy lifestyle. I'm going to follow a different lead. I'm going to chase a different prospect."

Even as Christians, we oftentimes still take the path that is most comfortable for ourselves. We measure our investment in Jesus Christ by how often our butts sit in the pew, or by the money we give to our church and charities. We read our Bible, memorize verses, and sing along with Christian radio to buttress our faith. We do the easy stuff. We do what makes us feel good about ourselves. Are we going to call that good enough? Is that as far as we're willing to go?

James wrote, "Faith by itself, if it is not accompanied by action, is dead" (James 2:17, NIV). That sounds like a call to action.

In Psalm 18:2 (NIV), David told us, "The Lord is my rock, my fortress, and my deliverer…in whom I take refuge." We have nothing to fear! Maybe we should put Bibles in the hands of those who may someday become believers, and let our actions "make the sale." Maybe we should go to the front lines where we are considered the infidel and introduce Jesus to people who may be hell bent on jihad. Maybe we should build a church where there are only a handful of followers, or sit with, and light the way, for those that are dying and alone. Perhaps we should step into the fire and see if there is someone that needs pulled out—someone that needs set free. Let's live reckless; let's poke the devil in the chest and say, "Do what you may, but we ain't backing down!" It may end in martyrdom, doing something dangerous sometimes does, but why not allow ourselves to line up with the Creator and fight? Not just talk about it. Not just support it, but actually take "the sword of the Spirit" and save souls from evil's clenched fist!

After Jesus walked on the water out to the boat filled with His disciples, He asked Peter to step out of the boat and come toward him. He may be asking us to do the same. If we're not afraid, and with enough faith, we can make that walk. Let's work miracles where we are a distrusted enemy, and speak His word where we are unwelcome. Let's do something dangerous!

> Now, Lord, consider their threats and enable your servants to speak your word with great boldness. Stretch out your hand to heal and perform miraculous signs and wonders through the name of your holy servant Jesus. (Acts 4:29–30, NIV)

With Dignity

Journal entry, November 14, 2014

What dignity looks like can be influenced by personal opinion. The Merriam Webster Dictionary gives us this definition for Dignity: The quality or state of being worthy, honored, or esteemed. If acting dignified is also considered being worthy, our view is definitely subjective. Only one man was truly worthy.

In the garden of Gethsemane, Jesus prayed about the death that He would be suffering through. "My Father, if it is possible, may this cup be taken from me. Yet not as I will, but as you will" (Matthew 26:39, NIV). Then a second time, Jesus prayed, "My Father, if it is not possible for this cup to be taken away unless I drink it, may your will be done" (Matthew 26:42, NIV). Then a third time, He prayed the same words. He accepted the Father's will. He accepted the struggle ahead—death on a cross—as an offering for each of us. In my subjective mind, that is how dignity should look. Accepting the will of God, no matter how it humbles us, no matter how it may affect us, no matter what His time frames, is living the definition of dignity.

Today, I learned about Brittany Maynard committing "suicide with dignity" as many news outlets referred to it as. I mean no disrespect to Brittany or her family, but I think that is called "quitting." If news sources are correct, Brittany suffered with an inoperable brain tumor for about nine months—after being given six months to live. I would agree that brain tumors are no easy fight, and further, the word "inoperable" should tell you the eventual outcome to most who suffer with this type of cancer. My brother, Charles, who is the toughest individual I have ever known, was given two months to live with the same type of brain tumor(s.) That was nine years ago. Yes, I said nine years!

Is being given two months to live, or six months, or a year, or two years, a death sentence? I suppose it could be considered that. It depends upon the resolve of the individual and the strength of those around them.

My work takes me in all different directions, and I always wish that I was home and able to visit my brother more. My point is that he is still here among us to visit. He hasn't given up. I don't think he ever will. There is no "quit" in him. Nor is there any quit in his wife, Cindy. They have not taken the easy path. Neither of them would ever consider suicide. Knowing full well that most suicides are due to mental health issues—completely forgivable in my subjective mind—this is different. In the case of willing and assisted suicide just to avoid the struggle ahead, my brother would consider that so very selfish.

Charles and Cindy know all about tough times. They know about chemotherapy and radiation combined. They know about chemo for four and five years straight without a break. They know about the trips back and forth to treatment centers, watching, while others they once saw there, aren't coming anymore. They know all about being humbled, and about burdens. They know about being dropped by their health insurance a couple of times. I can't begin to imagine the financial strains. There is a cost affixed to fighting. There is a price on suffering.

I remember when my brother married Cindy. Like any sibling I hoped for the best for my older brother and his new wife. How do you really know how a person or a marriage will turn out though? Cindy has proven to me the type of character she has. She has also shown the world how much she loves Charles.

The first years with cancer were scary and my brother was always sick and struggling. I can honestly say though, for the first four or five years, he never missed a day of work—not bad for a guy that was given two months to live. That's a testimony to what you can do when you refuse to give up. Was he sick and throwing up? "Heck yeah but that's no reason to miss work." That should give you some insight into what my brother is all about. Every year, every month, and every day has become tougher. Cindy has carried him for so long. She now takes him to her work daily because he is unable to care for himself. She feeds him many meals when he is unable. She is with him every step that he takes and most of those she supports his weight to steady him. Sometimes arms and legs work, and sometimes they don't. He cannot complete a sentence and sometimes cannot speak at all. He cannot bathe without help and support. She has no life of her own. Truthfully, his life is solely dependent upon hers. Just being able to go to the grocery means she will need a helper to sit with him while she is gone for a few minutes. For those that are close to them, we see the love in his eyes when he looks at her. Cindy is a true hero. My brother apparently knew that when he married her. I am amazed by how much two people can love one another.

Brittany Maynard gave up way too soon. Around year three of his battle, I asked Charles, "Why do you think God lets people get sick with cancer?" In the typical brilliance of my brother, he gave me an answer as if he had contemplated this same question before. He said, "You learn what you're truly made of when you have to fight for another day." A few sentences later, he expounded with, "God knows that cancer will bring people closer to Him." That stuck with me. I can attest that it does bring both patient and family closer to God. You realize that God is really all you have. He is hope.

I feel so sorry for Brittany Maynard's family. They lost someone they love. Unfortunately, only God knows how much time they lost with Brittany because she decided to avoid the struggle, and the pain, and "being a burden." She probably also missed the opportunity to make some heroes around her, or to be a hero to someone else that needed one. I am certain that many people who are fighting cancer look at my brother and say, "Hey…if Charles can do it, then maybe I can too." Or perhaps some caregivers look at Cindy and say to themselves, "I don't know how she does it, but if she can go another day, then I can too."

I have to ask, who really knows what tomorrow could bring? If tomorrow is the day that a breakthrough for that "inoperable brain tumor" is discovered, then Brittany made her decision a day too soon. Could she have given her husband and family another day, or month, or year of memories—chances to talk, chances to hang out together, chances to prove to the world what kind of heart they have? I am thankful for every day my brother fights and can give us. I'm so thankful for Cindy. I am convinced God put them together for this battle. My brother must have understood that this is about more than just him. No matter how or when it ends, he will never give up. He will only succumb on God's time and to God's will. This will define him.

Cindy exemplifies what it really means when you say "for better or for worse." When I think of angels, I think of her. The thousands of people that know them will have the standard set for them on how a battle with cancer is supposed to be fought—with dignity. When we fight sickness with every fiber of our being—like it's evil, the devil loses.

> And we know that in all things God works for the good of those who love him, who have been called according to his purpose. For those God foreknew he also predestined to be conformed to the likeness of his Son, that he might be the firstborn among many brothers. (Romans 8:28–29, NIV)

In hardships, we are transformed to be like Jesus. Because God loves us, he refines us through trials. By His will, He makes us worthy through Jesus Christ.

"In the same way, let your light shine before men, that they may see your good deeds and glorify your Father in heaven" (Matthew 5:16, NIV). God asks us to show others the way through our actions. He gave us breathe to get every drop of goodness out of those we love. If for no other reason, to prove that good is greater than bad, light is greater than darkness. Bad can be forgiven, but good glorifies the Creator.

"As each has received a gift, use it to serve one another, as good stewards of God's varied grace" (1 Peter 4:10, ESV). Fighting for another day, for God's will, for God's timeline, is using a precious gift. We should use all of the strength He has given us for His glory. It's our duty. When the day comes that we must "drink of the cup," as Jesus had to, then let it be for the sake of bringing those we love to the foot of the cross. If we can carry someone that needs help far enough that they can stand on their own, if we can bring out the best in others by being humbled ourselves, if we can be the reason that brings those we love closer to God, then we have done what God expects of us. Only then can we close our eyes with dignity.

Author's note: Charles was taken to heaven on January 24, 2015. Cindy was at his side when he met Jesus. He was a man of few words but of indescribable wisdom—a mechanic, a fire fighter, a first responder, a hard worker, and a believer. He was a loving and faithful husband to Cindy. He loved his family immensely. He was the best brother! We miss him, but we are comforted fully knowing that He is peacefully whole and perfect standing with Jesus!

Becoming an Imitator

In Ephesians 5:1–2 (NIV), we are told that we should "be imitators of God, therefore, as dearly loved children, and live a life of love, just as Christ loved us and gave himself up for us as a fragrant offering and sacrifice to God." How can we imitate God? We're to love as Christ loved us, giving his very life? As if that's not going to be difficult enough, Ephesians 4:22–23 (NIV) goes further, telling us to "put off your old self, which is being corrupted by its deceitful desires; to be made new in the attitude of your minds; and to put on the new self, created to be like God in true righteousness and holiness." This sounds almost impossible! Who can be like God in true holiness? Who can shine that brightly?

From Genesis to Revelation, much of the Bible can serve as a "how to" book for living life in a way that is pleasing to God. If you follow God's well designed playbook, "putting on the new self" will be like putting on your make up or pulling on your pants in the morning. Following His word will capture the very heart of God and reap a bountiful harvest of righteousness that will seat you next to Moses and Elijah at the banquet!

As a believer, Jesus Christ is already your Lord and Savior. He opened your eyes, ears, and heart, when you accepted Him. Paul wrote in Romans chapter 4 that, even though the devil has "blinded the minds of unbelievers," God said, "Let light shine out of darkness" and He "made his light shine in our hearts to give us the light of the knowledge of the glory of God in the face of Christ" (reference 2 Corinthians 4:6, NIV). This "light of knowledge" is our source for learning how we can become imitators of God and live the Lord's message.

Paul also wrote to the Galatians, "Since we live by the Spirit, let us keep in step with the Spirit" (Galatians 5:25, NIV). The followers of Christ are already at one stage or another of His transforming make over. Living by the Spirit is essential when building that temple for the Holy Spirit to dwell. "Keeping in step" will be as easy as breathing in His word. "I will put my laws in their hearts, and I will write them on their minds" (Hebrews 10:16, NIV).

> ...live a life worthy of the calling you have received. Be completely humble and gentle; be patient, bearing with one another in love. Make every effort to keep the unity of the Spirit through the bond of peace. (Ephesians 4:1–3, NIV)

> Do not let any unwholesome talk come out of your mouths, but only what is helpful for building others up according to their needs... (Ephesians 4:29, NIV)

> Be kind and compassionate to one another, forgiving each other, just as in Christ God forgave you. (Ephesians 4:32, NIV)

> Serve wholeheartedly, as if you were serving the Lord, not men, because you know that the Lord will reward everyone for whatever good he does... (Ephesians 6:7–8, NIV)

> Do nothing out of selfish ambition or vain conceit, but in humility consider others better than yourself. (Philippians 2:3, NIV)

> Do everything without complaining or arguing, so that you may become blameless and pure, children of God without fault in a crooked and

depraved generation, in which you shine like stars in the universe… (Philippians 2:14–15, NIV)

Set your minds on things above, not on earthly things. (Colossians 3:2, NIV)

Put to death, therefore, whatever belongs to your earthly nature: sexual immorality, impurity, lust, evil desires and greed, which is idolatry. (Colossians 3:5, NIV)

Rid yourselves of all such things as these: anger, rage, malice, slander, and filthy language from your lips. Do not lie to each other. (Colossians 3:8–9, NIV)

Make it your ambition to lead a quiet life, to mind your own business and to work with your hands…so that your daily life will win the respect of outsiders and so you will not be dependent on anybody. (1 Thessalonians 4:11–12, NIV)

God is sovereign and steadfast. He doesn't change but He certainly changes us. Paul wrote, "Therefore, if anyone is in Christ, he is a new creation; the old is gone, the new has come! (2 Corinthians 5:17, NIV)

As believers, we are transformed by and for Jesus Christ. If we delight in the Lord, His light will shine in our hearts. No matter what falls apart, He'll rebuild a magnificent temple from the rubble. Praise Him and He will draw alongside you. Humble yourself before Him and nothing in this world will cause you to buckle. He will build a fortress around you and uphold you.

Paul wrote in 1 Thessalonians 1:6–8 (NIV) to the "brothers loved by God" that "you welcomed the message with the joy given by the Holy Spirit. And so you became a model for all believers… The Lord's message rang out from you." Joshua was a man that "the

Lord's message rang out from." He was a mighty man of God, leader of the Israelites after Moses had passed. As Joshua led his people into the land that God had promised them, God caused the flow of the Jordan river to be "cut off and stand up in a heap" creating dry land for the nation to walk across (Joshua Chapter 3). God caused the walls of Jericho to fall with the blasts of trumpets and the shouts of Joshua's people (Joshua Chapter 6). God was asked by Joshua to stop the sun in the sky as they used the daylight to defeat the armies of the Amorites and "The sun stopped in the middle of the sky and delayed going down about a full day. There has never been a day like it before or since" (Joshua 10:13–14, NIV). If God can knock down walls, stop the flow of powerful rivers, and create an extra day by stopping the sun from crossing the sky, what good could you accomplish for God if "the Lord's message rang out from you?" Becoming a "model for all believers" and being made a new creation is His way of preparing us to do mighty works in His name. It's part of being set aside as God's chosen. Following His word and living by the Spirit readies us for God's plan to "let light shine out of darkness."

Paul's question in Romans 8:31 (NIV) was "If God is for us, who could be against us?" When we live His message: "No weapon fashioned against you will succeed, and you may condemn every tongue that disputes with you. This is the heritage of the LORD's SERVANTS, WHOSE RIGHTEOUSNESS COMES FROM ME, SAYS THE LORD" (Isaiah 54:17, CEB).

His Truth Is Marching On

What an incredible blessing that Simeon had received. "It had been revealed to him by the Holy Spirit that he would not die before he had seen the Lord's Christ" (Luke 2:26, NIV). Having been "righteous and devout," Simeon had been promised by our wonderful and holy God Himself that he would see the coming of the Lord, our Savior, Jesus Christ! What an amazing reward for loving our Heavenly Father!

Joseph and Mary had taken Jesus to the temple in Jerusalem to present Him to the Lord and to make an offering to the Lord, as was custom. The Spirit had summoned Simeon into the temple courts and it was there that they met. Simeon took the baby Jesus "in his arms and praised God, saying: Sovereign Lord, as you have promised, you now dismiss your servant in peace. For my eyes have seen your salvation..." (Luke 2:28–29, NIV).

> Then Simeon blessed them and said to Mary, his mother: "this child is destined to cause the falling and rising of many in Israel, and to be a sign that will be spoken against, so that the thoughts of many hearts will be revealed. And a sword will pierce your own soul too." (Luke 2:33–35, NIV)

Simeon saw the coming of the Lord. He held God's Glory and what would become the "living hope" in his arms. Peter wrote in 1 Peter 1:3–5 (NIV), "Praise be to the God and Father of our Lord Jesus Christ! In his great mercy, he has given us new birth into a living hope through the resurrection of Jesus Christ from the dead, and into an inheritance that can never perish, spoil or fade—kept in heaven for you, who through faith are shielded by God's power until the coming of salvation that is ready to be revealed in that last time." Simeon knew this was the beginning of salvation. Now, when you came before The Father, you would also be forever shielded by The Son and guided by the Holy Spirit. Glory! Glory! Hallelujah!

Julia Howe Ward must have thought of those verses about Simeon as she witnessed the troops in public review while visiting Washington DC. After seeing the soldiers marching in preparation for battle in the Civil War, she penned the famous and beloved war ditty, *The Battle Hymn of the Republic*. She apparently knew her Bible well, and like Simeon, her eyes had been opened, remembering his words, "My eyes have seen your salvation." Thoughts of the final battle between good and evil described in Revelation chapter 19 must have been an eerie comparison to the Civil War that stammered by her in parade. Her lyrics referenced Jesus's judgment of sinners, and the grace found in His forgiveness as if they were about to play out before her eyes. "Who is this robed in splendor, striding forward in the greatness of his strength? "It is I, speaking in righteousness, mighty to save" (Isaiah 63:1, NIV). One can surely believe that what moved her heart that day was in close comparison to what Simeon envisioned as he held the infant Savior, saying, "destined to cause the falling and rising of many," and "the thoughts of many hearts will be revealed." She must have fallen asleep that evening reverently believing that "mine eyes have seen the glory."

When reading *the Battle Hymn of the Republic*, it's evident that when Mrs. Ward was awakened that November morning in 1861, it may not have been the Civil War she had dreamt of and then wrote about. Although the Civil War was terrible and devastating, as we read her words, it's obvious that it was a different, even more significant war that she wished to bring to our attention. Perhaps overpowered by somber soldiers marching, she understood the grace in Simeon's reward, the eternal peace in knowing, with all certainty, the beauty of the coming of the Lord and His wonderful salvation. She sought His triumphant return!

Until that final day, His truth is marching on!

Battle Hymn of the Republic
Julia Howe Ward

Mine eyes have seen the glory of the coming of the Lord;
He is trampling out the vintage where
the grapes of wrath are stored;
He hath loosed the fateful lightning of His terrible swift sword;
His truth is marching on.
Glory! Glory! Hallelujah!
Glory! Glory! Hallelujah!
Glory! Glory! Hallelujah!
His truth is marching on.
I have seen Him in the watch-fires of a hundred circling camps;
They have 'builded' Him an altar in the evening dews and damps;
I can read His righteous sentence by the dim and flaring lamps,
His day is marching on.
I have read His fiery gospel writ in rows of burnished steel!
"As ye deal with my condemners, so with you My grace shall deal!
Let the Hero, born of woman, crush the serpent with his heel,"
Since God is marching on.
He has sounded forth the trumpet that shall never call retreat;
He is sifting out the hearts of men before His judgment seat;
Oh, be swift, my soul, to answer Him; be jubilant, my feet!
Our God is marching on.
In the beauty of the lilies Christ was born across the sea,
With a glory in His bosom that transfigures you and me;
As He died to make men holy, let us die to make men free!
While God is marching on.
He is coming like the glory of the morning on the wave,
He is Wisdom to the mighty, He is Succour to the brave,
So the world shall be His footstool, and the soul of Time His slave,
Our God is marching on.

The Short Speech

Paul's speech surely caused controversy. It ignited fierce hostilities. Paul had been preaching in Thessalonica and Berea where he had been met with strong opposition from the Jews. He had been creating new believers in the gospel of Jesus Christ, but along that same path, his successes had alienated unbelievers to the point of drawing up sides and inciting a riot. Paul was then whisked away by his followers to Athens and now was to speak before the Aeropagus.

The Aeropagus considered themselves to be what we today would call a "think tank." They enjoyed getting together and pondering things, considering the possibilities and relevance of ideas. It's likely they scoffed at most, but they were willing to listen to Paul and what he called 'the good news.' If for no other good and valuable reason other than to collectively doubt its validity, they wanted to learn more about this Jesus that Paul was spouting off about in the markets and synagogues. Perhaps they wanted to debate Paul's teaching or attempt to debunk it. After all, they were the thinkers of their time, an aristocracy of intelligence. Some philosophers who belonged to the group wished to further dispute what they called Paul's 'babbling,' so they took him before the Aeropagus. In what probably was considered by most to be a great honor, Paul had an opportunity to convince the "movers and shakers" of Athens, of the salvation found only in Jesus Christ.

It was a short speech. Paul hit them between the eyes.

> Paul then stood up in the meeting of the Aeropagus and said: "Men of Athens! I see that in every way you are very religious. For as I walked around and looked carefully at your objects of

worship, I even found an altar with this inscription: TO AN UNKNOWN GOD. Now what you worship as something unknown I am going to proclaim to you.

The God who made the world and everything in it is the Lord of heaven and earth and does not live in temples built by hands. And he is not served by human hands, as if he needed anything, because he himself gives all men life and breath and everything else. From one man he made every nation of men, that they should inhabit the whole earth; and he determined the times set for them and the exact places where they should live. God did this so that men would seek him and perhaps reach out for him, though he is not far from each one of us. (Acts 17:22-27, NIV)

Certainly, after just those few sentences, some spines grew straighter, and some butts moved closer to the front of their seats. After seeing all of the shrines and altars dedicated to so many different gods, even an "unknown god," Paul rocked their world with "there is just one God the Creator. Everything that ever was or will be is through His power and grace, even the very breath that fills your lungs and the impulses that cause your heart to beat."

Paul quickly concluded with:

Now he commands all people everywhere to repent. For he has set a day when he will judge the world with justice by the man he has appointed. He has given proof of this to all men by raising him from the dead. (Acts 17:30–31, NIV)

When they heard about the resurrection of the dead, some of them sneered, but others said, "We want to hear you again on this subject." At that, Paul left the council. (Acts 17:32–33, NIV)

Although the entire body of the Aeropagus was expecting a deep dive into Paul's teachings, Paul instead gave them the passionate "hit 'em where it hurts" version of the gospel of Jesus. There was no debate. There was only the quick and efficient truth. What the group of thinkers wanted to dissect and debunk, probably took Paul less than two minutes to say. Oh…they were still left to ponder the relevance of Paul's ministry; and still today, we see intellects of various sizes and shapes ponder what Paul so firmly believed. And yes, also today, some still snicker and sneer, while others want to be filled to the point of overflowing with the 'good news' of our Lord and Savior Jesus Christ.

When you're put on the spot or cannot seem to find the right words to quickly explain the gospel story, hit them between the eyes with Paul's eloquent version from Acts 17. Some will reject it, but you will also bring some listeners to their knees before Christ with it. Then, if they are clamoring to move from milk to solid food (reference 1 Corinthians 3:1–2), give them spoonfuls of Paul's writings in 1 Corinthians Chapter 15:

> But Christ has indeed been raised from the dead, the first-fruits of those who have fallen asleep. For since death came through a man, the resurrection of the dead comes also through a man. For as in Adam all die, so in Christ all will be made alive. (1 Corinthians 15:20–22, NIV)

Paul taught us that we don't have to fit in with the "movers and shakers." We don't need to ponder or debate. On the subject of salvation, we should not be tolerant. We have been given the truth. No one can ever change what we believe. We can boldly speak to others and our words will be impactful. We've been shown the way, the only way.

> And everyone who calls on the name of the LORD will be saved. (Acts 2:21, NIV)

We are

Most of us are familiar with the 2006 movie *We Are Marshall*. The movie is the story of how the Marshall University football team heals and rebuilds its team after a devastating, and heartbreaking, plane crash kills thirty-seven players, the vast majority of their coaches, trainers, and staff, along with many boosters. A true story, the tragedy crushed the community of Huntington, West Virginia, its hopes, and its spirit. After painfully rehiring coaches and then recruiting players, the program is forced to start from the very bottom, with nothing, and drag itself, along with the school, and the community's faith, back to the game. Newly hired Head Coach Jack Lengyel had to try to heal those who had lost beloved team and family members and also somehow inspire the entire campus and community to faithfully rebuild their hearts and believe again in something bigger than themselves. As the team finds its way, and as they manage to gain just a glimmer of respect on the field, a cheer begins to surface around the stadium, the school, and Huntington. "We are…Marshall. We are…Marshall. We are…Marshall." Day after day, game after game, they put grief and mourning behind them, and they find their way to victory. "We are…Marshall. We are…Marshall!"

Christians haven't created a cheer yet for our team. On most accounts, we are a quiet bunch. It shouldn't be in our nature to draw attention to ourselves anyway. Our play book is to humbly serve our loving God, giving Him the glory, and praising His name. We follow His path because we know where it leads. Day after day, game after game, we put sin behind us and we find our way to victory.

If we were Jack Lengyel recruiting players, what cheer would they hear when they visited our stadium on game day? If we kept it simple, like "We are...Marshall!" what would ours be? What are we? Who are we? What qualities would we cheer about?

In 1 Corinthians 4:10 (NIV), the apostle Paul labeled himself and fellow followers with "We are fools for Christ" followed by verses twelve and thirteen, "when we are cursed, we bless; when we are persecuted, we endure it; when we are slandered, we answer kindly." For Christians, this defines us in many ways.

Peter said that we "are a chosen people, a royal priesthood, a holy nation, a people belonging to God" (1 Peter 2:9, NIV). That sounds like an awfully good team to play for. It sounds as though we should rout all of our competition! We are...Chosen. We are... Chosen!

The apostle John told us that we are Christ-like when he wrote "We know that when he appears, we shall be like him, for we shall see him as he is. Everyone who has this hope in him purifies himself, just as he is pure" (1 John 3:2–3, NIV). We are...Christ-like! We are...Christ-like!

A few other verses tell us more about who we are as followers:

> We are hard pressed on every side, but not crushed; perplexed, but not in despair; persecuted, but not abandoned; struck down, but not destroyed. (2 Corinthians 4:8–9, NIV)

> ...we are his workmanship, created in Christ Jesus for good works... (Ephesians 2:10, NIV)

> ...(We) are a letter from Christ...written not with ink but with the Spirit of the living God, not on tablets of stone but on tablets of human hearts. (2 Corinthians 3:3, NIV)

> ...we are the temple of the living God. As God has said: I will live with them and walk among them, and I will be their God, and they will be my people. (2 Corinthians 6:16, NIV)

...(We are) sons, God sent the Spirit of his Son into our hearts, the Spirit who calls out, "Abba, Father." So you are no longer a slave, but a son; and since you are a son, God has made you also an heir. (Galatians 4:6–7, NIV)

We are therefore Christ's ambassadors, as though God were making his appeal through us. (2 Corinthians 5:20)

We are ambassadors. We are sons. We are heirs. We are the Potter's creation, the "work of His hand" (reference Isaiah 64:8). We trust in a God that we cannot see. We sleep in the lion's den and are not eaten. We are hidden in His heavenly power. We are safely set upon a high rock. We are givers of ourselves and what God has given us. We are steadfast martyrs. We are prayerful because we know God can change outcomes. We defeat nations with our sling and a stone. We are fearless as we walk through a fiery furnace. We are marked with His seal. We are loved. We are forgiven. We are his flock and He is our shepherd.

As God was talking to Moses from the burning bush (Exodus Chapter 3), God instructed Moses to go before Pharaoh and "bring the Israelites out of Egypt." Moses asked, "If I say 'the God of your fathers has sent me to you' and they ask me, 'What is his name?' Then what shall I tell them?" God said to Moses, "I AM WHO I AM. This is what you are to say to the Israelites: "I AM has sent me to you.'" (Exodus 3:13–15, NIV)

While Jesus defended himself against prying Jews in John 8:58 (NIV), He said, "before Abraham was, I Am." Also, in Revelation 1:8 (NIV), Jesus said, "'I am the Alpha and the Omega,' says the Lord God, 'who is and who was, and who is to come, the Almighty.'"

Our God Almighty is the "I Am," and since we are in Him, it is safe to declare our name as just simply "We Are."

We...are! We...are!

Taxes Paid

They say that there are just two absolutes here on earth: we will pay taxes, and we will die. That expression seems to hold true no matter what time or space in humankind we consider.

> After Jesus and his disciples arrived in Capernaum, the collectors of the two-drachma temple tax came to Peter and asked, "Doesn't your teacher pay the temple tax?"
> "Yes, he does," he replied. (Matthew 17:24–25, NIV)

In today's terms, Peter and Jesus were being audited! The kings of the earth have always collected taxes in some form. Whether for the common good or otherwise, since man first appointed government to oversee them, we've been contributing. In Moses's day, the Jews required the temple tax to maintain and secure the tabernacle. Then, in Jesus's time, the tax supported the temples. Tax collectors did just that—audited and collected.

> When Peter came into the house, Jesus was the first to speak. "What do you think, Simon?" he asked. "From whom do the kings of the earth collect duty and taxes—from their own children or from others?"
> "From others," Peter answered.
> "Then the children are exempt," Jesus said to him. "But so that we may not cause offense, go to the lake and throw out your line. Take the

first fish you catch; open its mouth and you will find a four-drachma coin. Take it and give it to them for my tax and yours." (Matthew 17:25–27, NIV)

For a carpenter, Jesus was an amazing fisherman. He knew where the valuable fish would be swimming! He directed Peter to take his pole, walk to the lake, cast a line, catch the first fish, and then pull the coin from its mouth. Peter then returned and paid the tax for both himself and Jesus with his catch.

Jesus posed the question, "Do the kings of the earth collect taxes from their children or from others?"

Peter answered, "From others."

Paraphrasing, Jesus resolved, "The children are exempt, but so that we don't offend them, we'll pay it anyway."

We are all children of God. "Yet to all who did receive him, to those who believed in his name, he gave the right to become children of God—children born not of natural descent, nor of human decision or a husband's will, but born of God" (John 1:12–13, NIV).

We're all a part of God's temple—His church. As Christians, we have all accepted that we owe a "temple tax" that has to be paid. It's a formidable amount. After all, we've been given His mercy and grace even though we didn't deserve it. Per Jesus, as God's children, we should be exempt, but to avoid offending anyone, Jesus put up the "Gone Fishing" sign and offered to pay the tax on our behalf. If we "believed in His name," and accepted His mercy, and His grace, and His forgiveness, He paid the price.

Near the beginning of His ministry, in the temple courts of Jerusalem, Jesus challenged the Jews, "'Destroy this temple, and I will raise it again in three days.' They replied, 'It has taken forty-six years to build this temple, and you are going to raise it in three days?' But the temple he had spoken of was his body" (John 2:19–21, NIV). The church isn't built of brick and mortar. It was built with the very essence that is God. He didn't need us to take care of an earthly structure. Jesus was the temple. Jesus is the Church. He wants us to worship what is the one true God. "For in Christ lives all the fullness of God in a human body" (Colossians 2:9, NLT). Jesus took all of our sins upon that same body and gave His life for us. He is the foundation of our faith. Paul wrote, "The life I live in the body, I live by faith in the Son of God, who loved me and gave himself for me" (Galatians 2:20, NIV). And "Now you are the body of Christ, and each one of you is a part of it" (1 Corinthians 12:27, NIV). We dwell in Christ, our church, and He dwells in us.

Jesus's fish and His coin paid the temple tax that day for Peter and Himself. Through His suffering and death on the cross, He paid for every single soul that chooses to belong to His church. He paid it with His life. Then, three days later, it was rebuilt! Raised again just as He said it would be. Our Redeemer reigns! Forever! Our Temple!

Heaven Opened

Kayla Mueller didn't play it safe. She gave everything she had for God, her price for being a disciple. On February 6, 2015, Kayla's life was taken from her while she was held captive in Raqqa, Syria, by an ISIS leader known as Abu Bakr al-Baghdadi. She had been held captive for a year and a half after being seized while leaving a hospital in Aleppo. She had been working with humanitarian groups in Israel, the Palestinian territories, and in northern India, giving aid to those in need. In late 2012, she felt a calling to help groups lending support to those fleeing war ravaged Syria along the Turkish border, a especially dangerous place for a white American female handing out food, supplies, offering shelter, and spreading the good news of Jesus Christ. Kayla wasn't picking the low-hanging fruit of those that are lost and needing to be shown the way, a daunting and treacherous calling all on its own. Kayla was entering through the very narrowest of gates. She was lining up each day against those raised up to naturally distrust Western Americans, mostly disrespect women, and lend very little credence to the salvation being offered through Jesus. She was a one-woman crusader showing love and kindness—a traveling revival tent coupled with caring, an outpost for restoring supplies, rescuing souls in need, and feeding hungry bellies and hopefully a few searching minds. Kayla was sowing seeds in "good soil."

Kayla was a student at Northern Arizona University and a member of United Christian Ministry. The Director of UCM, Kathleen Day, described her as "Christ-like" saying, "She did ordinary things with extraordinary measure." Near the end of her captivity, she and two others being held, both women, saw an opportunity for escape. Kayla weighed their chances for success and decided the two should go without her. She was afraid that her being too white and too

American could create an issue and eventually cost the other two girls their freedom or even their lives. Shortly after the others had escaped, Kayla was killed. She was twenty-six years old. ISIS claimed she was a victim of a Jordanian airstrike but no proof of that was found. Kathleen Day was right in her description of "Christ-like," but to simply correct her, Kayla "did extraordinary things as if they were ordinary."

In Acts 7:54–60 (NIV), moments before being martyred, it is described that "Stephen, full of the Holy Spirit, looked up to heaven and saw the glory of God… "Look," he said, "I see heaven open and the Son of Man standing at the right hand of God."

As reported by Raya Jalabi, news editor of the Guardian, "(Kayla) Mueller said that during her captivity, she drew comfort from her deep Christian faith, and in her words wrote: "I remember mom always telling me that all in all in the end the only one you really have is God. I have come to a place of experience where, in every sense of the word, I have surrendered myself to our creator because literally there was no (one) else + by God + by your prayers I have felt tenderly cradled in freefall." In the end, having surrendered herself to God, Kayla felt "tenderly cradled." One could certainly conclude that she, like Stephen, saw Heaven open and Jesus standing at the right hand of God!

Kayla didn't practice her faith from a distance. She could have stayed safely behind life's barriers, but instead, she consciously decided to put on her armor, leap over the barricade, and run into the physical and political crossfire to lend aid where it was needed. As reported by the Guardian on February 10, 2015, Kayla's aunt, Lori Lyon, said "Kayla has done more at her age than many people can imagine in a lifetime." She went on to add, "At a young age, she knew her calling."

> I am the good shepherd; I know my sheep
> and my sheep know me—just as the Father knows
> me and I know the Father—and I lay down my
> life for the sheep. (John 10:14–15, NIV)

Just as Jesus laid down His life for the sheep, Kayla laid down hers for the Lamb of God. So too, many of the early disciples of Jesus laid down their lives for the ministry. Through traditions and reliable historical accounts, scholars have generally agreed, for instance, that Peter was crucified upside down, as he emphatically stated that he did not deserve to be crucified in the same manner as Jesus. Paul was beheaded by the Romans. James was stoned and then clubbed to death. Andrew was crucified. Thomas was put to the spear as he professed the gospel to his killers. Matthew was stabbed to death. You get the idea. None of them played it safe. All of them gave everything they had for God. All of them were sowing seeds in fertile soil, and so, evil found and killed the messenger. Just like Kayla, they paid the price for discipleship.

We are reminded of how Jesus gave up his life for ours. In Romans 5:6–7 (NIV), Paul wrote, "You see, at just the right time, when we were still powerless, Christ died for the ungodly. Very rarely will anyone die for a righteous man, though for a good man someone may possibly dare to die." Kayla gave up her life for a righteous God, the same God that cradled her, and when she did, heaven opened.

Sources:

https://www.theguardian.com/us-news/2015/feb/10/kayla-mueller-letter-i-have-learned-that-even-in-prison-one-can-be-free
https://www.theguardian.com/world/2015/feb/10/family-kayla-mueller-confirms-aid-worker-killed

Why So Young?

Living a full life is not a given. Most of us probably pray for ourselves and those we love to enjoy long life, good health, and safety. When someone we know is taken from us early in life, we search for the reasons why. We consider what they had not yet accomplished, who they had not yet met, the events they will not attend, and "Lord, why at such an early age?"

We've all asked, "Why do the good sometimes die young?" It's a valid question because it's often true. We attend funerals for very good people that were too young to be called home. We stand and console one another by saying, "God takes the good ones young sometimes… I just don't know why."

In fact, God does sometimes take the good ones early. The prophet Isaiah said, "The righteous perish, and no one takes it to heart; the devout are taken away, and no one understands that the righteous are taken away to be spared from evil" (Isaiah 57:1, NIV).

Losing someone we love is like cutting away a portion of our own soul. It's a hurt that never heals until we see them again in God's kingdom. Until then, we have to trust that God knows when the time is right to harvest each of His believers. It may not make sense to us at all. It does to God though. He has perfect timing in everything He does. It may be as Isaiah stated: "the righteous are taken away to be spared from evil," or perhaps, they may have already accomplished the work that God intended for them. God can give one of us an entire lifetime of work that He needs completed, others though, may be among us only to accomplish one or two specific tasks. Jesus is an example of both dying at a young age, and also accomplishing the work that God sent Him to do.

> I have brought you glory on earth by completing the work you gave me to do. And now, Father, glorify me in your presence with the glory I had with you before the world began. (John 17:4-5 NIV)

Jesus was an efficient worker. His job was to set the foundation and also defeat sin and death forever. A tall task unless you are the Son of God. He finished His work, and then triumphantly went home.

In Psalm 31, David wrote about putting his time in God's hands. "But I trust in you, Lord; I say, "You are my God." My times are in your hands; deliver me from the hands of my enemies, from those who pursue me" (Psalm 31:14–15, NIV). Trusting God with our very lives, every detail, is what we are called to do. He knows what is ours to complete, and what lays ahead for us on this earth. He choreographs our steps flawlessly.

When we lose a loved one, we can find comfort in knowing that their unique beauty was a gift from our Creator. "He has made everything beautiful in its time. He has also set eternity in the human heart; yet no one can fathom what God has done from beginning to end" (Ecclesiastes 3:11, NIV). We may never know God's plan from beginning to end, but isn't it enough to know that those we loved played an important role for God, and that He found them beautiful in His sight? Then, because of the love that He had for them, our Father brought them to their heavenly home early!

Our hearts may ache for them. It's the worst kind of pain. Who are we though? If God has found them to be righteous and now wants to spare them from evil, what an amazing tribute! If they, like Jesus, have completed the work that God had for them, they have earned His amazing reward! If they trusted in God, putting their times in His hands, we should thank our loving Father for their answered prayer! If our Awesome Creator made the person we loved ideally beautiful in their time, and if He set eternity in their human heart, we should wipe away the tears from our eyes because there is no greater honor. When their beauty shines with such splendor,

He keeps them near. They forever reside in the inner circle of His immense power. They are His sunrises. They are His snowy peaks, His sandy beaches. It is those righteous ones that are taken from us early that become the wonder of His miracles and the glory that surrounds His throne!

The Beauty Contest

God created the heavens and the earth. Then, light. "God saw that the light was good, and he separated the light from the darkness" (Genesis 1:4, NIV). God then made the sky and the atmosphere, then the land and the seas. "And God saw that it was good" (Genesis 1:10, NIV). Then God made seed bearing plants and trees to cover the land. After that, he made the sun, the moon, and the stars, and laid out the entire universe. God said all of that was good too. The waters were made to teem with living creatures, and many birds were made to fly across the sky. Then, God filled the land with livestock, land dwelling animals, and wild beasts. All of those also passed God's inspection. Then on the sixth day, God created man, both male and female, and they were created in His own image—the image of God. And "God saw all that he had made, and it was very good" (Genesis 1:31, NIV). God said, "it was *very* good." He didn't call it "a good start," or say "It still needs a little work." He didn't say, "It's man's turn…let them improve on it." Instead, He declared His labor completed and then rested. He blessed that seventh day and made it holy.

In The Creator's eyes, we looked better than good. We looked "very good." After all, we looked like Him. It didn't take us long though before we errantly surmised that we could improve on His work, His image, and that our own looks and actions could somehow be more attractive. Appearance and achievements quickly became contested among ourselves. We discovered the body could be enchanting enticement for the senses. Our smile could be alluring. Our eyes could be irresistible. Our words could be seductive. We learned that "what we had" and "what we did" could draw attention from others, and we enjoyed the attention. Today, more so than ever, our human tendency is to believe we need to look good to be good.

We need to be beautiful for others to believe we are successful. We believe there has to be something attractive about us—something pleasing to the senses—before we can be found relevant.

We invest our faith and fortune in the image we project toward others. We wish to hide inside the walls of how others perceive us. Our never ending quest to make ourselves beautiful to the eyes of this world is born out of defiance toward God. The devil planted that seed. We fell for the deception. We believe we have to improve on what God created to grab attention for ourselves or to meet someone else's expectations. We attempt to make everyone we meet approve of what they see or hear from us; perhaps they'll want what we have? Our hair has to be a cool style or color, our complexion shining and vibrant, and our shape appealing since God didn't get it right. Our muscles have to be toned and bulging and our teeth brightly white. We hit the gym. We do our nails. We dress up that image in the most stylish clothes we can afford. We accessorize. We adorn it with shiny jewelry and polished rocks. We even ink graffiti on God's canvas and then roll up our pant legs and sleeves to show off the corrections we've made to His creation. We do "tucks," sucks, enlargements, reductions, lifts, plants, and who knows what other bodily fixes. We defile the once perfect and priceless masterpiece that was given to us.

We're constantly working to improve our standing in this world. We now live for our own personal satisfaction and tastes rather than for God's. We quietly, perhaps unknowingly, wish for others to envy what we look like, what we do for a living, how much we earn, and what we appear to have accumulated. We flaunt ourselves and our surroundings. We market our own personal brand.

We are enamored by those who walk the red carpet, those who wear designer dresses, and those with TV weddings. We want to be like them. That's our measurement for success. We often wish we could trade our lives for theirs. We worship them. Their image creates yearnings in us. "I wish I could be as pretty as her" or "If only I could afford to live in a house like theirs." If something looks better than what we have, we want it too.

Our sense of beauty and relevance is whacked. We've been hoodwinked by the devil. It's our spirit that is flawed, not our bodies or our appearance, not our standing or our value. We should not dislike anything about ourselves or what we have. Nor should we worship someone we believe may look better or have more. We should never covet what someone else flaunts. It's not worth our effort. That's not what is meaningful. Instead, worship God. He made us. He gave us life and everything else we have with it. We are created just as He intended—specifically made. God did his best work in us. Be His work of art. No need for improvements. "I praise you because I am fearfully and wonderfully made; your works are wonderful, I know that full well" (Psalms 139:14, NIV).

God gauges our beauty and our success differently than we do. The house we live in or the car we drive doesn't turn His head. He's not impressed by where or how we graduated. He doesn't care about our designer dress, or our hair, or our complexion. He's not looking at our smile, or our body mass index. He already knows what all that looks like. We are truly most desirable left exactly how God made us. "You are altogether beautiful, my darling, beautiful in every way" (Song of Songs 4:7, NLT). He created each of us in the beauty of His own image yet magnificently distinct, one of a kind. Back then, He said it looked "very good." We have to hope and pray today that He still feels the same way.

God knows beauty and relevance. He invented it. He intends to crown those "who walk in His ways," those who are not blinded by the darkness. He blesses those who put Jesus before their own ambitions. He lovingly touches us when we are wholly focused on Him, when we beg to do His will.

> For everything in the world—the cravings of sinful man, the lust of his eyes and the boasting of what he has and does—comes not from the Father but from the world. The world and its desires pass away, but the man who does the will of God lives forever. (1 John 2:16–17, NIV)

God's parameters will set the beautiful apart. It's His beauty contest. He'll decide which of us will be worthy and who among us will succeed. It won't matter what anyone else thinks.

When the eyes of this world judge against us, God finds us wonderfully precious.

When we are faithful, even when it costs us everything, God restores us.

When our relationship with Jesus Christ comes before all things, He sets us high upon a rock (reference Psalm 27).

When we draw attention to Him, instead of ourselves, God exalts us.

When we become like sheep walking among wolves for the sake of Jesus Christ, God empowers us (reference Matthew chapter 10).

When our hope and faith are laid naked, exposed for the world to see, God "gives us clothes of fine linen, bright and pure" (reference Revelation 19:7–9, ESV).

When we live each day understanding "He must become greater, I must become less," God is filled with joy! (reference John chapter 3).

In the end, it will be God who sees the true beauty and relevance within us. God will be the judge. He alone is mighty to save. He alone will crown His chosen winners.

If Souls Were Cash

In this era, the pitch man on any infomercial, or the front people pleading for sales on QVC or HSN, could find a way to sell ice to a penguin. A few good sales people are driven only by the thrill of "closing the sale," but let's be honest, the majority are in it for the money. They are either paid to sell or are executives in a company that is "For Profit." That aside, we have all worked in "sales." We may actually be sales people as a profession, or perhaps we have annual yard sales, or have sold a few of our own used cars, or have asked "would you like some dessert" while waiting tables.

Imagine if souls were cash. How hard would we work to win them? How good of sales people would we aspire to be then? The QVC and HSN networks always show us the unit sales rolling up in the corner of our television screen. Imagine if those were growing numbers of souls who had accepted Jesus into their lives, and we were counting up victories for our God—losses for the evil one. God would be excited about a new world wide TV network that we would call the "SON" or "Salvation Offering Network." Profits from the SON would only be counted up in treasures rather than cash. The bottom line would seem sparse by this world's standards, but the rewards would be 'heaven sent' and eternal.

Jesus's brother Judas, in Jude 23, asks us to "snatch others from the fire." As believers, followers, shepherds, and disciples, we all could consider those words an invitation to apply for the position of "sales executive" for the SON. Before sending your resume, consider the job description: "Sing to the Lord, all the earth; proclaim his salvation day after day. Declare his glory among the nations, his marvelous deeds among all peoples. For great is the Lord and most worthy of praise" (1 Chronicles 16:23–25, NIV).

The compensation package would certainly include much rejoicing, much gladness, vast treasures in Heaven, and endless life with our God who loves us beyond what we can imagine.

Every last one of us is qualified to assume this sales role. In the book of Acts, Paul and Barnabas explain how the Lord commands us with "I have made you a light for the gentiles, that you may bring salvation to the ends of the earth" (Acts 13:46–47, NIV). If the Lord has commanded us, then it would be proper to believe that He has also equipped us for the job!

We work very hard for money. Would we work just as hard for souls knowing the wages were lofty beyond belief? Jesus spoke to all of us in Matthew 16:24 (NIV), saying, "If anyone would come after me, he must deny himself and take up his cross and follow me." Perhaps we should all consider no longer selling ice to penguins, and begin selling the cross to non-believers. Then, watch our cups overflow!

Her Last Two Coins

God is a giver. He is willing to provide whatever we need! Jesus said, "Ask and it will be given to you; seek and you will find; knock and the door will be opened to you. For everyone who asks receives..." (Matthew 7:7–8, NIV). "If you, then, though you are evil, know how to give good gifts to your children, how much more will your Father in heaven give good gifts to those who ask him" (Matthew 7:11, NIV).

God gave us Jesus, His son, as an offering for our transgressions. God gave us the Holy Spirit to fill our hearts. God gave us a perfect planet to sustain life. God gave us the sun for heat and light and energy. God gave us days and nights. God made us in His likeness. God gives us air to breathe, hearts to beat, water to drink, fertile soil to grow food and feed livestock. God gives us minds and bodies to think and innovate with. God gives us hope. God answers our prayers. God is definitely a giver. Shouldn't we be like Him? Shouldn't we give to others too?

> Give, and it will be given to you. A good measure, pressed down, shaken together and running over, will be poured into your lap. For with the measure you use, it will be measured to you. (Luke 6:38, NIV)

Paul wrote in his second letter to the Church of Corinth, "Remember this: Whoever sows sparingly will also reap sparingly, and whoever sows generously will also reap generously" (2 Corinthians 9:6, NIV). Paul then explained in verse eight how "God is able to make all grace abound to you, so that in all things at all times, having all that you need, you will abound in every good work." Then in verse ten, "Now he who supplies seed to the sower and bread for food will also supply and increase your store of seed and will enlarge the harvest of your righteousness. You will be made rich in every way so that you can be generous on every occasion, and through us your generosity will result in thanksgiving to God."

The widow making her offering in Luke chapter 21 reveals to us what giving should look like.

> While Jesus was in the Temple, he watched the rich people dropping their gifts in the collection box. Then a poor widow came by and dropped in two small coins. "I tell you the truth," Jesus said, "This poor widow has given more than all the rest of them. For they have given a tiny part of their surplus, but she, poor as she is, has given everything she has. (Luke 21:1–4, NLT)

While the rest gave "a tiny part of their surplus" out of their wealth, the widow gave her last two copper coins. It was all she had. By this world's standards, it made no economic sense, but her wealth of faith was clearly evident. She did not worry if or how God would keep her. She didn't worry how she would be fed, or kept warm, or if she would have enough to retire, or if her financial decision would eventually erode her credit score. She had faith that God would provide everything she needed and more. She didn't need those two coins.

Giving is a test of faith. Giving beyond your means truly exhibits how much we believe that God will take care of our every need. If we give only from our excess, we're not passing the faith test. Jesus taught us in Luke 12:25-26 (BSB), saying, "Therefore I tell you, do not worry about your life, what you will eat or drink; or about your body, what you will wear. Is not life more than food, and the body more than clothes? Look at the birds of the air: They do not sow or reap or gather into barns, and yet your Heavenly Father feeds them. Are you not much more valuable than they?" God will provide. He'll even provide more then we need. No need to build bigger barns to store all that is yours. We can give freely and with a bit of extravagance.

Giving only out of our abundance shows God that we lack faith in Him providing. This may stem from us wanting to keep what we feel is ours, or it may be our attempt at self-promotion. We are so prosperous today, yet because we want so much, we always believe we have to earn more and keep more. We tend to always think of ourselves first. We hope that friends, family, old classmates, and future acquaintances will believe we are successful. We measure success by what we have—the home we live in, the car we drive, the designer labels we wear, or the price of the shades on top our head. Our hearts tell us that these will gain respect and approval from those around us. At the very least, we believe that our accumulated wealth brings us comfort and joy in knowing that we have enough. Yet we never really are satisfied. We always want to gather just a little more.

Joy does not come from the outward appearance of what we have achieved or how much we have amassed. Joy comes from what we have accomplished inside through our faith, from those "treasures we have stored up in heaven." We are truly admired when we lighten the yoke for others and show love to those in need. Our personal success is made visible by how our faith and our actions work together. "As the body without the spirit is dead, so faith without deeds is dead" (Read James 2:14–26). We can only truly be at peace by knowing we will be made perfect in Jesus Christ forever. When we are made perfect, there will be no need for wanting more.

The widow was successful. She had immeasurable wealth! A wealth of faith that could not be bought with any amount of money. We should admire her. Just two small coins can pay dividends much greater than we can imagine! If you give more than you should, God will give you life with such abundance that, no matter how hard you try, you won't be able to give it all away!

> A gift opens the way for the giver and ushers him into the presence of the great. (Proverbs 18:16, NIV)

The Measure of Greatness

"O, blessed father, let thy son's blood wash me from all impurities, and cleanse me from the stains of sin that are upon me. Give me grace to lay hold upon his merits; that they may be my reconciliation and atonement unto thee—That I may know my sins are forgiven by his death & passion. Embrace me in the arms of thy mercy; vouchsafe to receive me unto the bosom of thy love, shadow me with thy wings, that I may safely rest under thy suspicion this night; and so into thy hands I commend myself, both soul and body, in the name of thy son, Jesus Christ, beseeching Thee, when this life shall end, I may take my everlasting rest with thee in thy heavenly kingdom. Bless all in authority over us, be merciful to all those afflicted with thy cross or calamity, bless all my friends, forgive my enemies and accept my thanksgiving this evening for all the mercies and favors afforded me; hear and graciously answer these my requests, and whatever else thou see'st needful grant us, for the sake of Jesus Christ in whose blessed name and words I continue to pray, Our Father." (A prayer from George Washington's journal)

Every American knows the name of George Washington. From a very early age, we are taught to admire him as the general who carved out freedom for our country in the Revolutionary War and then became our first president. Given the timing in our nation's history, George Washington's feats are genuinely amazing but not necessarily surprising. His human ethics and devout longing for our nation to be free certainly helped propel him to revolutionary stardom.

It's difficult for us to imagine not being born an American. But those early revolutionaries obviously were not. They were subjects of Great Britain. Knowing the headstrong feeling of patriotism most Americans possess today, being known as anything other than "Americans" would nearly be inconceivable. Like those before us, many of us might choose death in battle rather than give up the freedoms that accompany such a title.

We have all known many characters who were nothing short of inspiring. But what really is the measure of greatness? Who ultimately decides who should wear that label? How does one earn that kind of consensus for admiration? Victory in war, success in business, an individual's ability to make unprecedented changes for the good of the people—all are reasons for proclaiming someone's greatness. It may not be for any one of us to decide though as mere humans. George Washington was driven by direction and ideals that were not from man but from God. Not only were his actions and life divinely inspired, but he was also protected by God. "You are my hiding place; you will protect me from trouble and surround me with songs of deliverance" (Psalm 32:7, NIV).

In 1755, as a young colonel in the French and Indian War, during an intense few hours of hard fought battle, Washington's duty was to carry orders from the generals to the officers on the battlefield. This required him to continuously ride between the enemy and his own troops under incredibly heavy fire, yet he was not wounded. Many opposing forces reported personally shooting Washington at point blank range and yet did not injure him. After the battle, in a letter to his brother, Washington himself admitted that something miraculous had occurred. In his words, "By the all-powerful dispensations of Providence, I have been protected beyond all human probability or expectation; for I had four bullets through my coat, and two horses shot from under me, yet I escaped unhurt, although death was leveling my companions on every side of me!"

As the general for the Continental Army, Washington would often be seen by troops in his tent, or in the woods, praying for guidance, shelter, and nourishment for his troops and also helpful intervention from Almighty God. "Praise be to the Lord, for he has heard my cry for mercy. The Lord is my strength and my shield; my heart trusts in him, and I am helped" (Psalm 28:6–7, NIV) He often told troops that victory and freedom were imminent as their endeavor was for the glory of God. He reminded them often that they were carrying out the will of a sovereign God, and that for that reason alone, there was no enemy that could defeat them.

In September of 1777, the British had marched to the outskirts of Philadelphia. Their forces included a group of British marksmen. One in particular was known to be their best sharpshooter, Captain Patrick Ferguson. Ferguson saw what appeared to be a high-ranking American officer traveling the trail in front of his men. He gave the order to fire at will upon the officer when his soldiers had open shots. Then, as quickly as the notion had come up, he felt an overwhelming knot in his stomach telling him that the ambush was not militarily acceptable, quickly rescinded his orders, and allowed the unsuspecting officer to pass without harm. The next day, he learned that the officer his team had in their crosshairs was Washington himself. He said later that he was suddenly emotionally struck with a sense of doing wrong and could not explain his decision except that some greater force told him not to hurt the officer.

There are many stories worthy of your own research that also signal God's righteous intervention in support of Washington's cause. On one such occasion, Washington and his army were starving as their supply lines had been blocked. They were camped along the Schuylkill River and trying desperately to survive on any food they could forage. Somehow, the river beside them warmed incredibly fast and early, melting far before spring, causing the fish to swim in frenzy beginning to spawn. A shallow bend in the open river provided a plentiful amount of fish to be netted, supplying an "all you can eat" scenario for the army that was so badly in need of food. Or research Washington's escape when surrounded on Long Island by a British force that was four times greater in size. Washington's troops were able to escape without being seen by a daring late night river crossing. Sources reported that there seemingly was no way the British could not have noticed them. Yet they continued to slip away a few row boats at a time until daylight. The entire Army was unable to escape by daybreak but was soon gifted by a dense fog which enabled their continued retreat. After the fog lifted, the British were astounded to see that their prey had somehow miraculously slipped away.

It is these types of actions and stories that immortalize George Washington in history. Are these also the same actions that elevate him to greatness? Most would argue an emphatic "yes" to that question. Christian's may contend, however, that it was the man's simpler actions that piqued the grace and love of God. Perhaps his obedience, humbleness, faithfulness, trust, and public admiration was the catalyst causing God to use Washington to give birth to a nation founded on Christian principles. Washington understood that a sovereign God was over all creation and he prayed for and relied upon His power and love to lend the needed direction and courage to forge a new nation. There are many examples of God using men to move humankind to follow Him—Moses, Joshua, David, John the Baptist, and Jesus, just to name a few. George Washington is another man, in a long history of men, who lived with the grace of God, and moved his people in the direction that God inspired forging the greatest nation in the history of the world.

To this day, although haunted by daily headlines of hatred and war, the United States of America is still a nation that does the work of God. As a Christian nation, our troops, missionaries, and average citizens of all walks of life, fight to further the same ideals as did Washington, and our revolutionary forces. Our nation is still filled with men and women who strive every day to further God's Kingdom, to teach others the gifts and responsibilities of freedom, and to exemplify the principles and ideology rooted in independence. We can sincerely believe that there are those walking among us today whose love and obedience to God has inspired His direction and personal protection. George Washington may have just been the first American to be protected by the power and glory of God. We can trust beyond all doubt that God is elated that we choose to be His followers but He is also hopeful that we will choose to be His leaders for a cause of immeasurable greatness!

> Yet their Redeemer is strong; the Lord Almighty is his name. He will vigorously defend their cause so that he may bring rest to their land… (Jeremiah 50:34, NIV)

Sources:

Washington's letter as published by the Encyclopedia Virginia in partnership with the Library of Virginia, www.encyclopediavirginia.org, LETTER FROM GEORGE WASHINGTON TO JOHN AUGUSTINE WASHINGTON JULY 18, 1755

Washington's prayer as published by the Christian Broadcasting Network (CBN) www1.cbn.com, originally from William J. Johnson, (New York: The Abingdon Press, 1919).

Amazed

> They went across the lake to the region of the Gerasenes. When Jesus got out of the boat, a man with an impure spirit came from the tombs to meet him. This man lived in the tombs, and no one could bind him anymore, not even with a chain. For he had often been chained hand and foot, but he tore the chains apart and broke the irons on his feet. No one was strong enough to subdue him. Night and day among the tombs and in the hills he would cry out and cut himself with stones. (Mark 5:1–5, NIV)

I assume that I am one of many, like the man Jesus met on the shore that day in the region of Gerasa. I have my demons. There are moments, and days, and weeks, and sometimes longer, where I live in "the tombs." I have tried to bind up my wrongdoings and subdue them. I'm not strong enough on my own to keep them tethered. I have tried to chain them, but they have always broken free. My sins have tormented me to the point that I have wished to cut them from my soul, from my mind, and heart. Night and day, I have cried out as I have traipsed through those tombs and throughout those hills and valleys.

> When he saw Jesus from a distance, he ran and fell on his knees in front of him. He shouted at the top of his voice, "What do you want with me, Jesus, Son of the Most High God? In God's

name don't torture me!" For Jesus had said to
him, "Come out of this man, you impure spirit!"
Then Jesus asked him, "What is your name?"
"My name is Legion," he replied, "for we
are many." And he begged Jesus again and again
not to send them out of the area. (Mark 5:6–10,
NIV)

Jesus knows my demons as well. He knows their name. I'm
sure what curses me has also knelt and begged Jesus, saying, "Please,
please, do not torture me, Son of the Most High God!" Yet knowing
their intentions were to tear my soul apart, I am comforted knowing
those demons were forced to beg Jesus for His mercy. Knowing that
evil trembled as it knelt before Him affirms His awesome sovereignty.
May His power forever punish them!

A large herd of pigs was feeding on the
nearby hillside. The demons begged Jesus, "Send
us among the pigs; allow us to go into them."
He gave them permission, and the impure spirits
came out and went into the pigs. The herd, about
two thousand in number, rushed down the steep
bank into the lake and were drowned. (Mark
5:11–13, NIV)

Jesus has authority over all evil. He casts out demons and strips
away sin. As He did for this possessed man who lived in the tombs,
He is ripping the wretchedness from my being as well. Jesus is washing me white with His own blood. He is hacking the detestable from
me and etching away the filth. I am being carved new by the power
and glory of His Holy Spirit!

Those tending the pigs ran off and reported
this in the town and countryside, and the people went out to see what had happened. When
they came to Jesus, they saw the man who had

been possessed by the legion of demons, sitting there, dressed and in his right mind; and they were afraid. Those who had seen it told the people what had happened to the demon-possessed man—and told about the pigs as well. Then the people began to plead with Jesus to leave their region. (Mark 5:14–17, NIV)

I am dressed and presentable to stand before God now. I am in my right mind. My thoughts and actions are no longer controlled by sin. Those demons will not convict me. Jesus alone has subdued them forever. I am being repurposed by the God who created me. He is replacing what was broken in me and piecing it together with what was good. I am reborn!

As Jesus was getting into the boat, the man who had been demon-possessed begged to go with him. Jesus did not let him, but said, "Go home to your own people and tell them how much the Lord has done for you, and how he has had mercy on you." So the man went away and began to tell in the Decapolis how much Jesus had done for him. And all the people were amazed. (Mark 5:18–20, NIV)

The Lord has certainly had mercy on me. I pray each day for God to use me in any way He wishes to build His kingdom. Whatever His will may be, I'm His. I believe that Jesus is asking all of His believers to "go home to your own people and tell them how much the Lord has done for you." I pray that He fills all of His followers with His Holy Spirit and we are directed in ways that will bind the world to Him. I pray He gives His faithful the strength to proclaim His message to those who are afraid, and that He plants our feet to stand bravely against those who "plead with us to leave their region." I pray that, through His power and mercy, "all the people" will find us "dressed and in our right minds", "amazed" by His love.

The Day of the Lord

> What the locust swarm has left the great
> locusts have eaten; what the great locusts have
> left the young locusts have eaten; what the young
> locusts have left other locusts have eaten. Wake
> up, you drunkards, and weep! (Joel 1:4, NIV)

God gave Joel a glimpse of what was to come. His words resonate about the mighty army of "locusts" unleashed by God that came and are truthfully still working here among us. As His faithful, we are called still to harvest "the fields" that are put before us, no matter how rich or laid to waste they may be. His faithful must scurry around among the "locusts," all the while keeping our hearts and hopes resting on He who is mighty and everlasting. It is a worthy battle for blessings and restoration!

> The fields are ruined, the ground is dried
> up; the grain is destroyed, the new wine is dried
> up, the oil fails. (Joel 1:10, NIV)

Joel foretold how the "harvest of the field is destroyed," and how "the joy of mankind is withered away." As the locusts eat their fill, our offerings to God are often lessened, muffled, and even kept for ourselves. The struggle of holding back the locusts takes all of the fight from our hearts. Believers can sometimes feel as though their faith is being emotionally scourged as Jesus was. It may be easier to wither and fall away.

Joel shouts a rally cry though! Grabbing us by both ears, he screams in our faces, "Declare a holy fast; call a sacred assembly.

Summon the elders and all who live in the land to the house of the Lord your God, and cry out to the Lord. Alas for that day! For the day of the Lord is near; it will come like destruction from the Almighty" (Joel 1:14–15, NIV). Remember who we serve! He created the universe and spun it all into motion! We are not going down in defeat! These "locusts" are about to be squashed by the weight of our awesome God!! He wielded them to shape our deliverance, and He will also "drive them into the sea!" In the end, those who call upon the Lord—*win*!

> Let all who live in the land tremble, for the day of the Lord is coming. It is close at hand—a day of darkness and gloom, a day of clouds and blackness. Like dawn spreading across the mountains a large and mighty army comes, such as never was of old nor ever will be in the ages to come. (Joel 2:1–2, NIV)

> Before them fire devours, behind them a flame blazes. Before them the land is like the garden of Eden, behind them a desert waste—nothing escapes them. (Joel 2:3, NIV)

> The Lord thunders at the head of his army; his forces are beyond number, and mighty are those who obey his command. The day of the Lord is great; it is dreadful. Who can endure it? (Joel 2:11, NIV)

Don't give up yet. There is hope, a way to safety. Joel's words may strike fear, but they also offer salvation. When we call out His name, we are nestled in the arms of a God who loves us!

> "Even now," declares the Lord, "return to me with all your heart, with fasting and weeping and mourning"... Return to the Lord your

God, for he is gracious and compassionate, slow
to anger and abounding in love... (Joel 2:12–13,
NIV)

Joel was begging Israel to repent during a time when the people
were turning away from God. A collision course was revealed to him,
and his people were on it. Today, those who have not found or refuse
to seek God, are on the same path. The ending won't be rewritten.
The path still leads to destruction.

Proclaim this among the nations: Prepare
for war! Rouse the warriors! Let all the fighting
men draw near and attack. Beat your plowshares
into swords and your pruning hooks into spears.
Let the weakling say, "I am strong!" (Joel 3:9–10,
NIV)

Swing the sickle, for the harvest is ripe.
Come trample the grapes, for the winepress is full
and the vats overflow—so great is their wickedness! (Joel 3:13, NIV)

God plans to gather the "multitudes in the valley of decision."

I will show wonders in the heavens and on
the earth, blood and fire and billows of smoke.
The sun will be turned to darkness and the moon
to blood before the coming of the great and
dreadful day of the Lord. (Joel 2:30–31, NIV)

And everyone who calls on the name of the
Lord will be saved; for on Mount Zion and in
Jerusalem there will be deliverance, as the Lord
has said, among the survivors whom the Lord
calls. (Joel 2:32, NIV)

Joel was harsh in his words for a reason. As much as they are pleading for repentance, they also cry out for revival. He gave us fair warning hoping we will line up on the "saved" side of the battle. Joel asked his people, and all of us who have followed since, to trust in God's promises. We can walk with Him into the battle of all battles without fear. He is a magnificent and beautiful force destined by Himself to rid this world of the unrighteous and to prepare His family for an incredible kingdom—the Holy City—where righteousness dwells.

Then they will go away to eternal punishment, but the righteous to eternal life. (Matthew 25:46, NIV)

The Everything Test

I saiah had a great vision in the year of King Uzziah's death. He saw the Lord seated on His throne. The Lord commissioned Isaiah with a paradoxical message for the wicked people of Judah and Jerusalem: "Be ever hearing, but never understanding; be ever seeing, but never perceiving. Make the heart of this people calloused; make their ears dull and close their eyes. Otherwise they might see with their eyes, hear with their ears, understand with their hearts, and turn and be healed" (Isaiah 6:9–10, NIV). It was God's intentions to separate the good from the evil, and the darkness from the light. From the day of Isaiah's message, there have been multitudes that are just too distant to hear, see, and understand the message.

The first disciples asked Jesus why he taught the people by speaking in parables. No doubt that the early believers then, and even new believers today, have found the exact meaning of Jesus's teachings challenging to understand. Jesus responded by saying, "The knowledge of the secrets of the kingdom of heaven has been given to you, but not to them" (Matthew 13:11, NIV). He continued, "Though seeing, they do not see; though hearing, they do not hear or understand" (Matthew 13:13, NIV).

Speaking in parables was the method with which Jesus sorted and sealed true believers. Perhaps for some, what the Savior was teaching wasn't interesting enough, or they were just unwilling to put in the effort to gain understanding. Although encrypted, the good made sense of it, but God had made it difficult for the wicked and sinful to find the message hidden in the parable. The good would understand. The lost would not.

"Who is it that conquers the world but the one who believes that Jesus is the son of God?" (1 John 5:5, NIV). If you believe that

Jesus is the Son of God, then the words that Jesus spoke will be easy to grasp. If they're not, you will joyfully ask questions, turn more pages, and study. You will seek Him and His Godly wisdom as if your eternity depends on it.

When you are seeking God, you are absorbing His word. Your eyes and thoughts are fixated on your Bible. You excitedly await church each week. You diligently surf the internet and radio for pastoral teaching. You're joining Bible study. You're attending workshops and conferences. You are pleading with God to give you more of the Holy Spirit! You just can't get enough. The act of seeking is worship! You will be immersed in His love and grace. Its satisfying indulgence is infinite.

Consider two lesser known parables spoken by Jesus, then, decipher.

> The kingdom of heaven is like treasure hidden in a field. When a man found it, he hid it again, and then in his joy went and sold all he had and bought that field. (Matthew 13:44, NIV)

> Again, the kingdom of heaven is like a merchant looking for fine pearls. When he found one of great value, he went away and sold everything he had and bought it. (Matthew 13:45–46, NIV)

These make perfect sense to those who have found the treasure—that perfect jewel—and refusing to let it get away from them, are willing to trade everything they have for it. It will be those that understand and those that turn and are healed.

We Too Will Be

From the moment we are born we begin dying. We will all pass away. That's not in doubt. It's what happens to each of us afterward that is in question. Theologians may disagree, but many believe that every single human soul will experience a resurrected life. As Christians, our faith is in our Living God Jesus Christ. The hope given us by His grace and mercy will be affirmed by His verdict from the throne.

> Come you who are blessed by my Father;
> take your inheritance, the kingdom prepared for
> you since the creation of the world. (Matthew
> 25:34, NIV)

Unfortunately though, some will hear, "Depart from me, you who are cursed into the eternal fire" (Matthew 25:41, NIV).

We know the way to everlasting life in God's kingdom. We should also know the details on resurrection and how and why.

> But someone will ask, "How are the dead
> raised? With what kind of body do they come?"
> (1 Corinthians 15:35)

God made Adam from the dust of the ground. He intended Adam and Eve to live with Him forever. Then sin entered into their bodies, their hearts and their minds. Sin brought death. Death came "through one man," Adam. There will not be a do-over. As death came through one man, so also resurrected eternal life came through one man, Jesus.

> "For as in Adam all die, so in Christ all will
> be made alive." (1 Corinthians 15:22, NIV)

In the book of Romans, the Apostle Paul wrote, "For if, when we were God's enemies, we were reconciled to him through the death of his Son, how much more, having been reconciled, shall we be saved through his life!" (Romans 5:10, NIV). God loved us enough that He sent His Son to die as an offering for our sinfulness. Just as sin brought upon the death of Jesus, God's love and grace gave Him resurrected life-our King forever! So, too, that same love and grace will also give those of us who love Him eternal life! Surely, God would not send His Son to die for anything less than our salvation—victory over sin and death!

Paul answered the complex question of the resurrection mystery in his first letter to the Church of Corinth.

> So is it with the resurrection of the dead.
> The body that is sown is perishable; what is
> raised is imperishable. It is sown in dishonor; it is
> raised in glory. It is sown in weakness; it is raised
> in power. It is sown a natural body; it is raised a
> spiritual body. If there is a natural body, there is
> also a spiritual body. (1 Corinthians 15:42–44,
> NIV).

We are of Adam's blood, borne of the same dust. We're perishable. Jesus was not of dust. He was heaven-sent raised up to reign forever with Father God. Jesus was imperishable. As dust, we will perish in weakness and dishonor. Our sin died with Jesus, and now reconciled to the Father, we also will be raised up with Jesus! We are raised by His awesome power and glory and brought before God imperishable! Hallelujah!

> So it is written: "The first man Adam
> became a living being"; the last Adam, a life-giv-
> ing spirit. The spiritual did not come first, but

> the natural, and after that the spiritual. The first man was of the dust of the earth; the second man is of heaven. As was the earthly man, so are those who are of the earth; and as is the heavenly man, so also are those who are of heaven. And just as we have borne the image of the earthly man, so shall we bear the image of the heavenly man. (1 Corinthians 15:45–49, NIV)

Our earthly bodies are dripping of sin but forgiven by grace. That which is perishable will be left to return to the dust, but our spiritual selves will be heavenly. Christ redeemed us with the offering of His own life. We are fully certified now to become "those who are of heaven."

Our sins were born from that very first sin. The first forbidden bite condemned each and every one of us.

> Consequently, just as one trespass resulted in condemnation for all people, so also one righteous act resulted in justification and life for all people. (Romans 5:18, NIV)

Jesus changed everything. Willingly dying on the cross for our sins, was the "one righteous act" that pardoned us from eternal death. We now bear the image of the heavenly man who has and freely gives eternal life in heaven!

> For just as through the disobedience of the one man the many were made sinners, so also through the obedience of the one man the many will be made righteous. (Romans 5:19, NIV)

> Listen, I tell you a mystery: We will not all sleep, but we will all be changed—in a flash, in the twinkling of an eye, at the last trumpet. For the trumpet will sound, the dead will be raised

imperishable, and we will be changed. For the perishable must clothe itself with the imperishable, and the mortal with immortality. When the perishable has been clothed with the imperishable, and the mortal with immortality, then the saying that is written will come true: "Death has been swallowed up in victory." (1 Corinthians 15:51–54, NIV)

Death will come for all of us. For believers in Jesus Christ, and His resurrection, death is just where eternity begins. We should be fearless, bordering on eager. When that trumpet sounds, we too will be no longer of dust, but of heaven. We too will be raised in His power and glory. We too will be clothed in His image! We too will be made forever alive in Jesus Christ!

About the Author

Ken Kilgore is a resident and native of LaGrange, Indiana, and has been a member of Emma Church in Topeka, Indiana, since 1998. Ken works in sales and marketing for a regional oil and energy company, and along with his wife Mary, owns and operates two small businesses. Ken enjoys journaling and writing along with their two dogs in his spare time.

CPSIA information can be obtained
at www.ICGtesting.com
Printed in the USA
FFHW022235310119
50363057-55464FF